Tobias Endler

After 9/11:
Leading Political Thinkers about the World, the U.S. and Themselves

17 Conversations

Barbara Budrich Publishers
Opladen & Farmington Hills, MI 2011

A CIP catalogue record for this book is available from
Die Deutsche Bibliothek (The German Library)

© 2011 by Barbara Budrich Publishers, Opladen & Farmington Hills, MI
www.barbara-budrich.net

ISBN   978-3-86649-364-3

Verlag Barbara Budrich ⓑ Barbara Budrich Publishers
Stauffenbergstr. 7. D-51379 Leverkusen Opladen, Germany

28347 Ridgebrook. Farmington Hills, MI 48334. USA
www.barbara-budrich.net

Cover Photo Credits: From left to right: Robert O. Keohane; Michael Novak; Joseph S. Nye, Jr.; Clyde V. Prestowitz, Jr.; Zbigniew Brzezinski; Jean Bethke Elshtain; Benjamin R. Barber; Strobe Talbott (© Katherine Lambert); Noam Chomsky (© Donna Coveney, MIT); Cornel West (© Brian Velenchenko); Francis Fukuyama; James M. Lindsay; Nancy Soderberg; John Bolton; Michael Walzer; Anne-Marie Slaughter; Howard Zinn (© Roger Leisner, The Maine Paparazzi, Radio Free Maine)

Jacket illustration by disegno, Wuppertal, Germany – www.disenjo.de
Typesetting: R + S Beate Glaubitz, Leverkusen, Germany
Printed in Europe on acid-free paper by paper&tinta, Warsaw

After 9/11:
Leading Political Thinkers about the World,
the U.S. and Themselves

for J.
who saved me

Contents

Preface

Thirty years ago, French philosopher Michel Foucault famously pronounced the intellectual dead. The United States of today proves him wrong. And while the nation's leading thinkers engage in a vital and extensive debate, it is not a new debate. In fact, it was reignited forcefully in the aftermath of September 11, and it has not subsided ever since. Participants in the discourse differ widely, and they don't shy away from conflict. They cover the entire political spectrum. All of them prominent figures in American public life, they include renowned academics and members of think tanks, political advisers, former and current members of government, authors, and journalists. Following the terror attacks, they have published their respective points of view, their attempts at explaining what happened, their suggestions what to make of it – always intent on reaching out to the broad educated public, and at times even far beyond their original sphere of influence.

To what end?

The best answers will be provided by the public intellectuals themselves. During a Research and Teaching Fellowship at Yale University in 2007/08, I conducted seventeen interviews from a specifically designed questionnaire. While the reader can thus compare various individual positions on single issues, each conversation also takes its own turn. As a whole, the transcripts capture an illuminating snapshot of the environment America's professional thinkers are facing at the start of the 21st century. Each one has carefully established a public persona, and each one deserves recognition for their professional achievements. All of them defy rigid classification. Yet it was something else that turned each conversation into a unique experience: My interviewees' charisma and openness to dialogue. Occasionally, their persuasive power was startling, and I found myself intrigued by their company although I strongly disagreed on the subject. More than anything else, though, what will stay with me was their contagious curiosity about the world.

In 1980, Foucault had remarked that "more and more is being said about intellectuals, and I don't find it very reassuring." Here I will let them speak for themselves.

Acknowledgments

My intellectual and practical debts in regard to this project are profound and finally unrepayable. Ultimately, *After 9/11* owes the most to the seventeen thinkers who agreed to share their thoughts with me. Yet many others have provided substantial support throughout the project. Each of them, in his or her own way, helped me to achieve my goals.

My supervisor, Dietmar Schloss, devoted considerable time and energy to improving the organization and content of my manuscript. His substantive contributions and years of experience sharpened my analysis and leavened my prose, and I am grateful for everything he has done.

I have been able to draw on the experience of several of my colleagues and teachers, who have done their utmost to point me in the right direction. First and foremost, Martin Thunert provided valuable information and feedback, as well as helping to set the ball rolling for the book. For their suggestions and for allowing me to bounce ideas off of them, I would like to thank Detlef Junker, Mischa Honeck, Florian Pressler, and Elena Matveeva of the Heidelberg Center for American Studies (HCA), John Lewis Gaddis and Seyla Benhabib of Yale, Jeremi Suri of the University of Wisconsin-Madison, Stephen Wayne of Georgetown University, John Owens of the University of Westminster, Alastair Hamilton of the Warburg Institute, London, and Jagoda Marinić.

Styles Sass, Michael Shiels, as well as two unknown brave readers from Yale's Writing Center and Heidelberg's Graduate Academy ensured that my grammatical and typographical errors didn't make it into the published text.

Sumi Jessien and Barbara Budrich provided key editorial advice in structuring the final manuscript. I am also grateful to them for copyediting. My agent, Swantje Steinbrück, was as good a critical reader of my manuscript as she was a guide through the decisions involved in negotiating a book contract. I appreciate everything that they and their staff have done to make *After 9/11* a reality. Thank you also to the HCA for generous financial support.

Finally, I would like to thank Jagoda, my partner, my critic, my love. You taught me to believe in this.

Introduction

Rebuilding began only three days after the shock. With the ruins of the World Trade Center still burning, as they would continue to do for weeks after, and the smoldering rubble of what used to be the West's most significant symbol of economic wealth strewn across lower Manhattan, the bulldozers took up their work. The scale of what had happened was not yet comprehensible. Still, the first traces of 'Project Rebirth' were already under way.[1] New York City, shaken by a terrorist attack of unprecedented magnitude, had been in a state of paralysis, but was far from dead, and began to stir again beneath the pall of smoke and ash which had hovered over it for days. As Rudolph Giuliani, the city's mayor, put it: "Tomorrow New York is going to be here. And we're going to rebuild, and we're going to be stronger than we were before..."[2]

Ten years later, walking down Church Street from the north toward the site where the Twin Towers dwarfed everything else before two hijacked airplanes appeared out of a clear blue sky to bring them down, what meets the eye is a vast gaping space. With the debris cleared away, the stark barren plane is still as much a wound as it is a building site. But from amidst the bustling clatter the construction cranes protrude. Ground Zero is the place to watch the stricken American giant getting to its feet again.

Since that fateful day in the fall of 2001, however, the United States has not been merely rebuilding the famous skyline of its gateway to the world. On a less visible level, another, very different kind of reconstruction has been taking place. Over the last nine years, the nation has been

---

1   An initiative of the same name chronicles the reconstruction work at NYC's Ground Zero. http://www.projectrebirth.org, retrieved 03-20-2010.
2   Eric Pooley, "Mayor of the world", *Time*, December 31, 2001.

going through a process of ideological reorientation. The war in Iraq, to this day still not a 'mission accomplished', has further intensified this process.[3] And just when things started to get back to normal, the nation had to cope with another shock: the most severe financial crisis since the Great Depression. Compared to the terrorists' attack, the crash on Wall Street in the fall of 2008 meant a blow from the inside, and together, these events have considerably shaken both American self-confidence and Americans' trust in their government. The crisis is far from over; the nation has not yet found its bearings. This holds true even though many find fresh hope in Barack Obama's election as the 44th President of the United States. *New York Times* columnist Timothy Egan summed up the high expectations set for the new administration:

> This was the first real 21st-century election – rejecting the incompetence of the Bush years [...] and the poison of media-driven wedge politics. As a nation, we rejoin the world community. As a sustaining narrative, we found our story again.[4]

The United States, the most powerful nation on the planet, has a remarkable record of re-defining its relationship with the world community. More significantly, it also has a remarkably successful record of recovering quickly from crises. The American "narrative," however, is still strained by the traumatic experience of September 11, and a feeling of insecurity and vulnerability – unfamiliar to a nation that thought itself beyond the reach of its enemies – persists. Yet America is gradually recovering, and it is being assisted in the process by one specific group of citizens: its public intellectuals. They have mounted a significant effort to help heal the wounds incurred on September 11. While aware that the scars inflicted on that day will remain on the nation's soul, America's intellectuals consider two cures to be indispensable: explaining the past and construing the future for their people. Thus they have entered onto the public stage again, and very determinedly so. Their ideas become influential because they manage to reach political and religious organizations, the business community, and educational institutions which then disseminate the message further (while making it more palatable). In addition, the intellectuals themselves are well versed in using the main-

---

3 George W. Bush (in)famously used the term in his speech aboard the aircraft carrier *USS Abraham Lincoln* on May 1, 2003, declaring combat operations in Iraq to be over.
4 Timothy Egan, "This American Moment – The Surprises", *The New York Times*, November 5, 2008. http://egan.blogs.nytimes.com/2008/11/05/this-american-moment-the-surprises/?em, retrieved 11-05-2008.

stream media as a platform, an amplifier and a distributor in this process. Even those parts of the public who do not pay attention are thus eventually affected – if only indirectly by the political decisions inspired by these ideas.

In this book, seventeen of America's most important public intellectuals present their views on their nation's role in the post-9/11 world. They also present their views regarding their own role in American society. While coming from different professional backgrounds, they are all experts in foreign policy and engage in a vibrant, comprehensive debate. Howard Zinn, Francis Fukuyama, and Joseph Nye are all at home in academia, but they live in different worlds with regard to their political preferences. Anne-Marie Slaughter, James Lindsay, Nancy Soderberg, and Strobe Talbott share similar views on a range of issues. All of them have ties to the academic world, yet Talbott now heads what is arguably America's most influential think tank, while Slaughter joined the Obama administration. It is safe to say that John Bolton and Cornel West have little in common beyond their U.S. passports – at least politically. On a more personal level though, the Conservative hard-liner and the free spirit from Princeton – who has recorded his own hip-hop album with Prince and KRS-One – share a marked preference for anecdotes, featuring George W. Bush and Snoop Dogg, respectively.

The conversations with Bolton and Benjamin Barber took place the same day, separated only by a 30-minute walk down Fifth Avenue, yet the statements made were far apart. Both men have turned their backs on academia though, and the latter, just like Clyde Prestowitz, has founded his own think tank. Noam Chomsky, at odds with most views held in academia, nevertheless remains a faculty member at MIT, where he intends to stir controversy well beyond his recent 80th birthday. Robert Keohane, dressed in a tracksuit and returning slightly late for the interview from his daily cycling workout around the Princeton campus, proves a patient and amiable interlocutor. So does Michael Walzer, who feels that inviting the interviewer for lunch beforehand is in order. Jean Bethke Elshtain offers to help find the best flight connection to Chicago where she teaches. Zbigniew Brzezinski, a contemporary of Chomsky, gets straight to the point (and straight out the door) since, as an advisor to Obama, his time is limited. Michael Novak, *éminence grise* of the American Enterprise Institute who has a private website, takes the time to inquire about the interviewer's family.

What all of these professional thinkers have in common – besides their enigmatic personalities – is their commitment to respond to the state of their nation. Irrespective of their political preferences, they regard it as their task to both analyze the mistakes of the past and provide a plan for the future that they hope might prevent their nation from blundering again.

Public opinion is an elusive phenomenon, and in a country as big as the United States, different people are always going to be affected differently by a myriad of issues – which, in addition, are in constant flux. Still, a number of issues rise above the rest since they relate to events that everybody feels have changed their lives. That horrendous morning of September 11 is undoubtedly such an event. People's perceptions of their nation and the world were fundamentally shaken and the old system of values no longer holds. In search of orientation, the public embarks on a journey of recovery, re-thinking, and re-evaluation. Public opinion is more receptive than ever to the voice of experts – some of whom reinforce the status quo (advocated by parts of the Conservative camp), while others are committed to renewal and change (exemplified by Obama's campaign slogan 'Change We Can Believe In'). The opportunities are immense – the tragedy lies in the calamity that triggered them.

Public intellectuals have seized this rare chance to consolidate and strengthen their position in society, and act once more as a decisive factor in shaping public opinion. Since 2001, the book market – which traditionally boasts a sizeable current-affairs section – has been flooded with publications on American foreign policy. They are generally marked by an accessible, down-to-earth writing style, which renders them both comprehensible and appealing to a larger public. More often than not, a catchy title highlights the agenda, promising the customer sophisticated reading pleasure and a refinement of one's foreign policy knowledge. Intellectual loyalty to this mode of publication – the book – is striking, given the omnipresence of modern means of communication such as web forums, blogs, podcasts, newspapers, and magazines. However, authors (including the ones interviewed in this book) have implied that – especially when compared with the transitory electronic medium – books provide lasting, scientifically sound, and verifiable knowledge by renowned experts on the subject – in other words, a 'reality-check' on the innumerable statements floating around on the Internet. That doesn't mean that America's intellectuals neglect other media and restrict themselves to the comparatively lengthy process of voicing their opinions in a book every year or two. Commentaries, op-ed articles, reviews, and interviews on the subject abound in all major newspapers, and intellectual magazines cover the entire political spectrum.[5] They bear witness to the extent that the current debate is geared toward the broad, educated public.

Discussion thus takes place in the public sphere, a forum that is, at least potentially, accessible to all. Obviously, it is the privilege of a limited number of established protagonists – eminent *literati* – to interact with a growing audience. Some of them have by now attained the status of celebrities, and they seem to enjoy the comforts of fame. Traveling the country on extended book tours, gracing TV shows with their expertise, they are brilliant minds with a devoted following.[6] Occasionally, some of them succumb to the temptation and play to the grandstand. Others will change their mind on a specific issue only to defend their new position just as vehemently as the one held dear not long before. In any case, these opinion-leaders address the American people directly in search of support for their points of view. They therefore feel the need to adapt their style and approach to the task at hand, i.e. to boil down complex foreign policy issues and explain their implications to (and for) the ordinary citizen. Academic heavyweights in their professional lives, these public intellectuals are prepared to compromise some of their standing among their peers in order to reach out to a larger audience beyond the ivory tower.

The debate is also public in yet another way. Contributors themselves are interrelated. Constituting an informal network, they constantly respond to each other, acting and reacting within the boundaries of what can be regarded as a sub-genre in the field of current-affairs books. Interplay takes place in the form of critical reviews as, for example, in a recent

---

5   Readers face a large selection: From the Conservative *National Review* (founded by William F. Buckley in 1955), *National Interest* (1985), and the recent *American Interest* (2005), to moderate and liberal magazines like *The New York Review of Books* (1963), the venerable *New Republic* (1914), *Foreign Affairs* (1922), and *New Yorker* (1925). More on the fringes are the Neoconservatives' organ *Weekly Standard* (1995), and the leftist *Nation* (1865) or *Dissent* (1954), to name just a few. Most of these magazines have a comparatively – at times surprisingly – small circulation. They make up for this by their respective formats, which are tailor-made for their specific audiences. Since their readership is extremely interested and engaged in politics, and since they have a loyal following in the crucial circles of the political establishment, they exert considerable influence.

6   Cornel West has managed to bridge the seemingly unbridgeable gap between the Ivy League and Hollywood, appearing in both the second and third part of the science-fiction blockbuster *The Matrix*. Epitomizing the phenomenon of blurring boundaries, West simply played himself; his character is named 'Councillor West'.

issue of the *New York Review of Books*, where the author tackles the issue of (American) empire by comparing five contrasting publications on the subject.[7]

This public debate is the response of America's intellectuals to the growing demand by the well-educated and influential sectors of the public to understand their nation's current role on the global stage. As members of the media, the political establishment, and the business community, they bring these issues to the attention of the broader public. As a result, a growing number of Americans want to know what their 'men and women of letters' have to say about a whole host of current issues such as, what led to the catastrophe of September 11? How best to prevent a similar catastrophe, and how best to restore America's damaged reputation – without sacrificing the nation's exceptional standing? What to expect of Obama? How to become once again the *city upon a hill*?[8]

Still, the nation's leading thinkers did not wait around for a jump-start from the public. In fact, most have been trying rather vigorously to reclaim the spotlight for themselves. They feel a need to position themselves – to sharpen their profiles – so as not to become increasingly irrelevant, pushed aside by growing competition from political journalists, Internet bloggers, and a host of television and radio experts (the so-called *pundits* such as Ann Coulter, Bill O'Reilly, Michelle Malkin, Glenn Beck, and Rush Limbaugh). The best way to remain in the public eye is to set up one's stage in the nation's square. Today's intellectuals have done exactly that. By initiating, steering, and perpetuating a national debate on America's future, they discuss and define their nation's role in a world that has changed since September 11.

---

7   See Alan Ryan, "What Happened to the American Empire?", *The New York Review of Books*, Vol. 55, No.16, October 23, 2008.

8   In 1630, John Winthrop warned the Puritan colonists who were to found the Massachusetts Bay Colony that their new community would be a 'city upon a hill', watched by all the world.

After 9/11:
Leading Political Thinkers About the World, the U.S., and Themselves

17 Conversations

Benjamin R. Barber

Distinguished Senior Fellow at Demos, New York City
President and Director of CivWorld at Demos
Walt Whitman Professor of Political Science Emeritus,
Rutgers University, NJ

Q: Dr. Barber, what audience do you have in mind for your publications?

B: There are five audiences, very broadly speaking.

One is the broad academic audience, the audience one reaches when one publishes an academic book, or in a professional journal such as the *American Political Science Review*. That is the audience that any scholar will aspire to reach. It is the audience of those who speak across the academy. But it is still quite narrow, it is professional and technical. Within it, there is a second, still narrower audience: The technical specialist audience. A political scientist who works, say, on comparative government in Burma. Basically, the specialist here speaks only to other specialists who study and care about Burma.

The third audience is the lay audience of intelligent, cultured, thoughtful Americans. They have some sense of and they help define intellectual life in America. You could probably categorize them as readers of *The New York Review of Books*, people who read at least one or two weekly opinion magazines, on the Right *The Weekly Standard*, or the *National Review*, on the Left *The Nation* or *The American Prospect*. They probably also read *The New Yorker*, and watch public television, and of course they read a daily newspaper – less than half of America does nowadays! That is a much broader audience that goes way beyond the academy. The people from this third arena are likely to constitute your fan base – if you have one.

The fourth audience is 'politically engaged America', the people who vote, which is only half of the nation.

The fifth audience is not an audience at all really, since it consists of the people who don't vote, who don't read newspapers, who don't even watch national television news, they only watch local news, if at all. That non-audience you can just forget about. Even if you publish an op-ed piece in *USA Today*, they are not going to read it. If you go on the *Bill O'Reilly Show*, they are not going to see it because they simply don't follow anything. And that is already half of America. They are not engaged in public life in any meaningful sense.

Almost all 'public intellectuals' reach the third audience, the audience that lies just beyond the academy. They may be musicians, politicians, journalists, lawyers, or doctors, but they take a civic interest in following public life. The first target of any public intellectual is to move from the specialist community of the academy into that more encompassing audience – that is by far the most important move. The fact is very, very few academics make even that jump. But for me, I am particularly concerned with moving from the third to the fourth circle. That fourth spectrum – they do vote, they are somewhat engaged in public life, they come late to public elections, but they do follow things – I am trying to reach because they are the ones who determine American votes, and they are the ones most vulnerable to persuasion, if they can be gotten to listen. They are most in need of edification, whether by me or others. This circle is the most difficult and challenging target audience, but in a way the one I most cherish, which is why although about half of the things I do are university-related, I am much more interested to go speak to the High School Social Studies Association of America, or to a union conference, or a corporate retreat because that is where the future of the country is going to be debated and determined.

Q: Especially regarding this fourth circle, is there an aspect of 'public schooling', or an educational component, involved in what you do?

B: Here is the tragedy: That 'schooling' of this fourth wider public is actually the responsibility of the media, the so-called 'fourth estate'; informing citizens, giving them a civic foundation for thinking in public terms about public affairs, allowing them to be encouraged to think critically and independently. The media has a civic responsibility. But because our media are corporate-owned and profit-driven, their interest is primarily in entertaining and pandering to that public, not educating and helping form them. As a result, television does the very opposite of what it should be doing, it actually encourages the most trivializing and reductionist forms of public debate. We have seen this in this extraordinary primary campaign, in which what somebody's preacher may have said in some inflammatory quotes becomes the campaign. That is not the candidates' doing – they are human, they may have said some silly things – but it is the media who grab the silly things and ignore the real issues.

So just when here in the United States we have a negative savings rate, when the American trade deficit is incredibly high, when the dollar is at an all-time low among all major currencies, and when a lot of countries have stopped even looking for American leadership, we witness a primary campaign focused on trivial, irrelevant matters that fail to address the coming crisis – which, however, the newly elected President Obama would have to confront face-on! That is not the candidates' fault because they have in fact tried to come back to core issues and principles. But the media don't permit it.

To come back to your question, the people who ought to be mediating public deliberation and educating the public for democratic debate are precisely the media! But they are precisely part of the problem, and not part of the solution.

Q: One of the very first sentences in the introduction to your book, Fear's Empire, *reads: "America is failing to read the message of mandatory interdependence that defines the new twenty-first-century world." Why did you choose to focus on foreign policy?*

B: This is a great example because even when the debate gets serious in politics, it is about the price of oil, about jobs, about consumerism and spending, about health or welfare policy. In the American case, it is almost entirely domestic. The amount of time in any American presidential campaign spent on foreign policy is tiny, and yet most of the issues, including the ones I just named, cannot be intelligently thought about in the absence of the international, the interdependent context. And that parochialism calls up endless pandering. Both major Democratic candidates, Clinton and Obama, have been going around Michigan, Ohio, and Pennsylvania saying "we will bring the jobs back." That is a flat-out lie, and they know it. There is no way those jobs are coming back, it is not in the power of the president even if they wanted to bring them back. Almost immediately after Barack Obama was elected, it became apparent that a dire free fall in employment would be the real challenge! The interdependence of the economy, the flight of capital, the free movement of labor and manufacturing capital means that it is just not in the power of a President of the United States to fix the economy within American frontiers without addressing the global crisis. Not anymore. But because of the obsession with domestic policy, politicians talk exclusively in these terms.

My effort here, my message in this particular book was: Terrorism in the United States finally allowed Americans to say: "Wait a minute, maybe what happens abroad counts, maybe we better understand the world better, maybe we have got to train and enlist the help of Arab speakers and understand what is going on in the Middle East." But because of President Bush's focus on war and unilateralism, that cosmopolitan concern lasted half a year, and then people went back to the same: "Let Bush fight the war on terror, and – as President Bush himself had counseled the American people – let's go back to the mall." An awareness of that crucial interdependence that defines the modern world was missing in the Bush administration and is absent in the policy debates among candidates in the current presidential campaign; and almost never mentioned in the media. The media insist self-servingly that this is because Americans don't care about foreign policy. But it is the other way around: The leadership of the media is supposed to insist: "We know you don't care, but you need to care, and here is why you need to care."

Q: What is the balance of power like between the world of 'thinkers' – academia – and the world of 'doers' – the world of practical politics?

B: Neither the government nor the academy have very much power. The real power lies with the media. When I am teaching, I have a student three hours a week. The high school teachers altogether have a student twenty-five hours a week, thirty weeks a year. The Internet, video games, television, and movies – all those multiplying pixels – have young people in their grasp sixty hours a week, fifty-two weeks a year. They are the real tutors in our society. They shape the American mind – which was what I was talking about in *Jihad vs. McWorld*. They shape the American political debate. The politicians don't. Barack Obama spends a great deal of time trying to elevate the discourse, saying "let's talk on a higher level," and Hillary is accused of being a policy wonk, but at least she wants to talk about policy. But the media have not permitted that to happen.

So what is the relationship between the experts in the academy and the politicians, regarding their influence on the public mind? Neither have a lot of influence. The academics who – like me – want to have a public influence have to find a way to get into the media and be heard in the media. And the politicians desperately need the media. But if the media want to turn the Obama campaign into the Reverend Wright campaign, that is what they will do. And they can label me, distort me or ignore me as they please.

Q: Is it the need to be heard that is behind your decision to choose the think tank – neither the academy, nor the government?

B: A little bit, yes. I have been in the academic world for forty-five years. I didn't spend my career in this intermediate space of think tanks and policy institutes. But having spent a lot of time in the academy, now that I am older, at this point in my life, I feel the academy is more an obstacle to than a facilitator of having an impact on debates, helping to shape debates. It was time to move on, it felt like the academy was beginning to limit my capacity to talk to people in those circles beyond the university. But it is also true that I have always insisted on trying to stake out a position somewhere between the pure expert and the paid policy person. I have never taken a paid job with government. My five years as a Clinton advisor were spent as an outsider – he never paid me, but the result was I kept my own voice, I kept my freedom. And that was true for the work I have done with other leading political figures as well, both here, as with Howard Dean, and abroad.

To some extent, the position I have chosen at Demos, in a think thank and policy institute – a "network for ideas and action"– as well as with my own NGO CivWorld, which sponsors Interdependence Day, is trying to stake out a position where I don't lose my academic and professional credentials, but where I am freer and better able to speak easily to a wider public. And not to get a paid position as a consultant because then I would become a partisan, an ideologue – somebody whose first job is to sell the product of whomever they work for, not to offer them unbiased counsel.

Q: Looking back over history, the American intellectual seems to have lived with a certain tension from the beginning. On the one hand, there is the need for critical distance to allow for comparatively unbiased judgment of society. On the other hand, there is a desire to intervene in that very society. What do you make of this claim to act somewhat outside of purpose-driven constraints, given the fact that the majority of intellectuals today are affiliated with the academy, the government, or a think tank?

B: What you say is very accurate, and it does capture a deep tension. It goes all the way back to Plato. Plato went to Syracuse, thinking "maybe I

can actually persuade this tyrant, Dionysus II, to modulate his policies."
He was deeply disappointed and almost got himself killed. Machiavelli
thought he was going to be the advisor of Lorenzo di Medici, John Locke
and Rousseau had similar ambitions. If you go down through the history
of political theory, you will find a great many people who were understood to be brilliant, objective, detached scholars who nonetheless, to
some degree, crossed the line, attaching themselves to and trying to serve
the powerful. They did so earnestly, but perhaps foolishly, in thrall to the
double illusion that a) the powerful would really listen to them, and b)
somehow their ideas, if heeded, could shift history's course.

There is always a degree of risk, an element of vanity. That is always
the case. I can excuse myself, saying I knew the risks, and forgive myself
the vanity. I never took money. I had no illusions about the fact that we
were likely to have very little influence, and I even wrote in my memoir
The Truth of Power that for advisors to be ineffectual is probably a good
thing because the president alone got elected, and he alone is the one with
the responsibility and the legitimacy. But at the same time, it is true that
one harbors some pride and vanity which makes you think that maybe
there can be at least one instance where you can change the face of things
just a little bit. I have a relationship with Gaddafi now in Libya, consult-
ing with him over the past few years. On the one hand, he is the longest
reigning autocrat on earth, but on the other hand, I take his theorizing in
The Green Book of direct democracy seriously, and he appears to like and
even listen to me. This cannot help but generate tension. Does it compromise your ability to speak out honestly, and forthrightly, and to represent truth to the larger public? Possibly. Any public intellectual who says
that they have no interest in power, they are just there to tell the truth, is
lying. To be a public intellectual is to crave some degree of influence.
Otherwise, one can just refuse to be a public intellectual, just go and do
your scholarly work.

There are some scholars who inadvertently end up having a great deal
of influence: In *The Theory of Justice*, John Rawls had a profound effect
on how we think about the distribution of justice. But any of us who go
outside of the academy and speak in a more public way – of course we
want to affect and shape affairs, and shape public opinion, and elite opinion as well. And if you want to shape elite opinion, one way or the other
you need to have relationships with the elite and with the power they exercise, and that distorts your view. In the 1980s, I wrote a very critical

review of Arthur Schlesinger's book *Cycles of American History* in the *New York Times*, which he never forgave me for. In it, I said that in the end he became an inferior historian because of his attempt to justify his relationship with the Kennedy administration, and to make Kennedy look better than he was. He was still furious when he dismissed me in his memoirs. I think he was inventing a myth, his views as a historian had been distorted by his participation in and the attempt to shape the Kennedy administration's legacy. But now perhaps I have done the same in 'serving' President Clinton and counseling Muarmmar Gadaffi. Perhaps this is Schlesinger's posthumous revenge.

Q: A more recent period of history – commonly referred to as postmodernity – carries a preeminent notion of relativism: A universal truth is virtually non-existent, or at least hard to pin down. Still, as the author of a book like Fear's Empire, *you would certainly claim validity and truth in what you have to say...*

B: I am not a postmodernist. I am too old and fustian, and in fact I have been a staunch critic of postmodernism; I suspect it has run its course and likely exhausted itself. The problem with postmodernism is that in terms of its philosophical purposes, it is an abstract critical theory, but the theory is hard to sustain in practice. Last year, I wrote a piece in *Ethics* on my friend William E. Connolly's latest book in which he vigorously advances a postmodernist thesis, and at the same time asserts his credentials as a leftist Democrat. But you can't really do that. It ends up making a hash of the theory, or making his political views seem arbitrary. Postmodernism has never been sustainable as a practice. It works as critique but action cannot rest on critique which in fact it obstructs.

Richard Rorty has always had Connolly's problem. Rorty was a brilliant postmodernist philosopher, but at the same time an ardent liberal, progressive Democrat, and trying to balance those two stances turned him into something of a contortionist. I don't have that problem but only because I don't buy the postmodernist position theoretically, and remain willing to assert something like objectivity or intersubjectivity. At least my political positions are not hamstrung from within and I can share Connolly's and Rorty's politics without feeling like an epistemological hypocrite.

Q: Taking one last step toward the present, would you say that the authority of intellectuals has increased since September 11, possibly due to a demand on the side of the public for a guiding voice of reason that will ex-

plain the course of their nation to them? If so, the notion of decline in the intellectuals' influence and importance – as put forward by Hofstadter, Bauman, and Posner, among others – would have to be challenged...

B: Do you think it is possible that both statements are true? Which is to say, in certain ways, the role of public intellectuals has deteriorated – that is partly the fault of the media, it is partly the fact that a lot of intellectuals are partisans and deeply engaged in justifying one side or the other of a polarized debate rather than assuming that truly independent stance that gives the public intellectual credibility. In that sense, there has been this kind of decline, what Julian Benda long ago called a "betrayal of the intellectuals, *la trahison des clercs.*"

But on the other hand, there are certainly plenty of intellectuals around, there is no dearth of public speakers. Paul Berman is a good example: Take his controversial *Terror and Liberalism.* I think he is utterly wrong in his attack on Islamicists as new totalitarians and make my argument in my essay on Hannah Arendt in a forthcoming anthology. Yet Berman certainly has plenty of influence.

To those who insist public intellectuals have vanished, one can cite Voltaire who once said about Rousseau quite brilliantly: "Rousseau denies the greatness of modern civilization, and talks about the corruption of modern philosophy, yet his own critical savaging of intellect is the proof of his argument's weakness." Richard Hofstadter wrote decades ago about the anti-intellectualism of American life and the declining role of intellectuals in it, yet Hofstadter is one of the great intellectuals everybody reads. It is the same thing with Posner and Bauman. The very people who are making this argument disprove it because by virtue of their making the argument, and having it widely heard and discussed, they are the counterfactual for what they are saying. If what they claimed were true and intellectuals went unheard today, you wouldn't even be aware they had claimed it. So both things are true. There is some slippage in the status of intellectuals, yet they are omnipresent, their discourse growing more polarized and corrupt.

I would like to think – it's not always true – that being immune to typecasting via some ideological or political frame is part of what it means to be a successful public intellectual. I take some pride in the fact that people can't quite figure me out. I write about Edmund Burke approvingly, and I write about Michael Oakeshott admiringly, but I disdain William Buckley and detest William Kristol, the editor of the conservative journal *The Weekly Standard*. In the cornucopia of encomiums following his death, even Liberals forgave Buckley his rancid politics, and his reactionary ideology, and even his racism apparently because of what a charmer and gentleman he was. But to me being difficult to classify ought to be the mark of an honorable public intellectual.

Q: What does your audience expect from you? Concrete policy proposals, or rather a visionary framework for American ideals?

B: It is hard to tell, and here is why: The success or failure of a book to appeal to this or that audience is powerfully constrained by the very media through which a book must make its mark.

For example, I thought *Fear's Empire* was an important and trenchant book. It was mildly prescient, written before the war in Iraq, yet predicting much of what happened. But on the whole, the foreign policy establishment paid little attention. I do not belong to the establishment, I am not Robert Kagan or Richard Haass, the President of the Council on Foreign Relations. The people who needed to certify that it was at least an interesting and important argument mostly ignored it. The general media took it up, and the public took it up. But in the absence of that 'official' certification my argument didn't become part of the debate within the foreign policy establishment. There was a time when a number of people complained that only the Right and only the establishment were represented on the Council on Foreign Relations, and at that time they invited a small number of people like me to become members. But a book like *Fear's Empire*, which to me was as prescient and as useful as *Jihad vs. McWorld*, got paid relatively less attention because – why? The foreign policy establishment was unwilling to give it serious consideration? Because I am hard to classify? Because I am not a foreign policy specialist, and haven't served in the State Department? These can just be excuses, yet it is often the case that public intellectuals will write books that get ignored or maligned by the professionals to whom they are addressed.

Jack Beatty – a long-term serious magazine editor and very fine amateur historian – wrote a book about 19th-century wealth. A really good book for the general public which was an attempt to talk about the production and corruption of wealth in the 19th-century that might allow us to understand 21st-century inequalities of wealth. But because he is not a professional historian, the historians refused to take the book seriously, and although it was a fairly serious book, it didn't get the attention it

needed to get, and did not become part of the subsequent debate about
American inequality.

Well, a writer takes his lumps, and too much special pleading won't
help. But what does annoy me is when people today say: "Well, in 2003,
nobody understood what the stakes were, we all believed President Bush on
WMD, so of course we all voted for the bill enabling the war." Excuse me,
some politicians understood well enough and voted no, and I wrote a book
– without being inside, without reading the intelligence reports – that was
pretty clear about the flimsiness of the rationalizations for and the likely
consequences of a war in Iraq. Trouble is, of course, to the extent you succeed in being beyond partisanship, you deprive yourself of a sectarian and
partisan bullhorn that allows your voice to be amplified and heard. Robert
Kagan is a darling of the Right, and any time he writes something, or did
during the Bush administration, you knew all the rightist writers and the
media were going to jump on it. And if Noam Chomsky makes an argument, there will be certain people on the Left who will be all over it. But if
you can't quite be classified in party or partisan terms, that's a problem.
This happened to Michael Oakeshott here in England, one of the greatest
political philosophers of the 20th century, a Conservative, and certainly a
Tory, but a philosopher who was a genuine independent and who called it
the way he saw it. Funny story about Oakeshott, with whom I studied: He
was invited by William Buckley to come to the 40th anniversary dinner of
the *National Review*. Everyone thought "terrific, Buckley's landed the
greatest living British Conservative." Except Oakeshott refused to be type-
cast, and once at the *National Review* lectern ended up pillorying the *National Review* crowd. They left dinner in disarray, appalled that they had
invited him. He was an independent thinker, and he hated the knee-jerk
style of right-wing American thinking in the 1970s. They couldn't believe
it, and they cried: "But surely you are one of us! How dare you not parrot
our views?!" The sign of a public intellectual is finally to listen to no voice
but your own. Of course, your own voice is going to be shaped and influenced by lots of other voices, you won't be able to resist being pulled in
certain directions, but nonetheless your first job is not to ask: How will this
affect my political constituency, my philosophical constituency, my university, my party? But: Is this a clear and fair view of the subject, inasmuch as
I am able to render it?

Q: How do you evaluate the importance of morality in politics? Is it the task of an authority somewhat above the shoals of everyday politics to watch over the moral aspects of it?

B: Yes, as long as we construe the term 'moral' in a very broad way. There are obviously moralistic – which is usually a pejorative for moral – ways of narrowing, and condemning, and judging in a biased manner. But if by 'moral' we mean disinterested, an appeal to larger standards, standards that move outside of party, outside of particular academic disciplines, then I think public intellectuals are moralists. Harold Laski and more recently Michael Walzer have done that on the Left. I don't think, by the way, that William Buckley did that on the Right, but Michael Oakeshott did. There is a moral tone.

Another standard to which public intellectuals have a responsibility is history. People talk about the post-9/11 terror period as if the Cold War never existed. They don't go back and examine the strengths and weaknesses of deterrence policy and the resonances to be found there for what was to come. That is one of the things I do in *Fear's Empire*. Looking at 19th-century American foreign policy, it becomes evident that the condemnation of Bush for moralizing is overdone: I exonerate him from the charge of being the only president to use the language of self-righteousness and virtue. Exceptionalism goes all the way back: Americans have spoken a language of unique virtue in defending American foreign policy all the way back to Washington. It is absurd to think that it is just Bush indulging in righteous arrogance.

Part of what an intellectual does then is to appeal to the standards that are disclosed by and distilled from history. When you do that, you have a foundation for non-partisan clarity because you have the authority of having understood and seen the past and offered it as a standard for evaluating the present. It allows you both to criticize Bush, but also put him in a setting where he is not just some solitary idiosyncratic idiot who got everything wrong, but someone instead who partakes in a long if dangerous tradition. Seeing that tradition, and why he is part of it, and what he is appealing to, yields a kind of moral authority. Also if you pull away from the interests of a particular constituency or party, you are in a better position to adduce arguments that – to the extent they have a moral flavor – reach into something deeper than the special interests of one class or another. So it is not that you have to be a moralist in that narrow sense of coming from Christian, or Islamic morals, or from a utilitarian position. It is critical thinking itself that backs off from interest and rebuffs special classifications that yields that moral authority. If you have read Plato, and Aristotle, and Machiavelli, and Rousseau, if you have read Marx, Weber, Oakeshott, and all the others on both sides of the question, and they perch in your head as you write, if you are – as Machiavelli said – engaged in a conversation with the dead every time you pick up your pen, there is a kind of authority because you don't just speak for yourself. It is not the magazine you are writing for, it is not the party you are speaking for, but rather you are channeling an old and enduring tradition of debate. I don't ask what Hillary Clinton or Obama are going to think about what I write, I wonder what Machiavelli, or Max Weber, or some of my teachers – Oakeshott or Karl Popper or Ralph Miliband or Judith Shklar, all dead but, oh, how alive – might have thought about it. And that means when I speak I speak not just for myself with earnestness and sincerity, because so does the teenage blogger, but that I am writing through a set of filters; and those filters are thinkers, philosophers, teachers who go all the way back, all the way down. As you know, this is not a voice very popular in this culture. Some may tolerate it, but many will mistake it for arrogance, or trivialize it as dropping names. They don't know what it means to spend a life among books with which you engaged in a lifetime conversation. In a postmodern, relativist age where the authority of great thinkers carries no weight, it will seem pompous or peculiar. But for those who recognize the authority of the voice, it is neither arrogance nor antiquarianism but simply a way of life, a way of thinking.

Q: Let's take the issue of morality to the international level of foreign politics: Is there a general consensus across political affiliations that the American version of democracy should be disseminated throughout the world? And that any controversy is mainly about how to proceed with this dissemination most effectively? A quote from the chapter 'The War of All Against All' brought up this idea: "If taken seriously [...], the appeal to democratization as the rationale for Pax Americana in Iraq and elsewhere can bring liberals aboard President Bush's battle cruiser."

B: Yes, you are exactly right. It is a correct reading. Part of the point of this book is to say that while Bush has made a mash, a disaster out of democratization, he is actually part of a long historical tradition that goes back to the Puritans' City on the Hill, America as having special strength, exceptional virtues, a providential destiny. Liberals and Conservatives alike who have talked about American influence in the world recognize this model exceptionalism. Even now Democrats are saying we should stop trying to impose democracy with soldiers, and just put our historic democratic virtues on display: the election of President Obama!

The argument I am trying to make is although America is an interesting and important model of one approach to democracy – and a very healthy one – there are many different forms of democracy, and many roads to reaching it. The notion that democratization means Americanization is counterproductive in two ways: a) it is not true, and b) given that America has – under Bush – had a bad reputation, it taints democracy's good name and will lead to its rejection by others. I am part of the consensus inasmuch as I do believe – unlike the old Realists and cynics – that democracy ultimately is the way of the world. That all human beings are capable of freedom, all societies are capable of some form of self-government. But where I differ is in insisting the possible forms of freedom and self-government are radically different from society to society, from culture to culture. There are many different ways of seeing and understanding democracy. While I agree with those idealists who think the whole human race is capable of and has a right to liberty and self-government, the roads are so various that for the United States to in any way suggest others must look something like us to become free, or that they have to listen to us to grasp democracy is a deep mistake. It is one of America's greatest mistakes. Our strongest influence has come when we have been doing the least in the name of democracy, and the most *as* a democracy. Not because that says 'imitate our model!', but because it proves that if we as a complex, multicultural people are capable of it, then others in their own way are capable of it as well.

Q: Still, how important is it that the United States remains the sole superpower? To quote from your conclusion: "Other nations cannot pursue preventive democracy in the absence of American participation or in the presence of American hostility. Is America up to the challenge? Hard to know."

B: The reality is American hegemony, even in a world after sovereignty. We are much further down the road to the end of sovereignty than we were seven or eight years ago. But here is the great irony: America remains not only the most powerful nation in the world, but probably has more unilateral, hegemonic power than any other nation before. During the Cold War, we had a bi-polar balance. But with the collapse of the Soviet Empire, despite the rise of China, the United States now exercises a cultural, military, and economic power unparalleled in history. On the one hand, the most powerful hegemonic nation in history under conditions that are unipolar, not multipolar; on the other hand, a nation that may have less usable power than any that has come before in this interdependent world. At one and the same time, we have more power than ever, but that power is less capable of shaping the world unilaterally than ever before. The situation we are in is that unless we find ways to collaborate and cooperate with friends, neutrals, and even enemies, despite our grand power we are not going to be able to prevail. We still have a great deal of power, but whether it is used for good or ill, whether it is used to block the interdependent collaboration that is needed, – which is what Bush did – or to further those agendas: that is the issue.

Fareed Zakaria's new book makes the argument: The world wants us to lead, but if not, get out of the way! What I am saying is: It is not so easy for us to get out of the way, and it is not so easy for the world to push us out of the way because we still remain, as nations go, extremely powerful. So the real question is: Can we create constructive forms of interdependence, constructive forms of collaboration in which a hegemonic power now becomes a partner of many other peoples? My work takes up these questions: What does an interdependent paradigm look like that is democratic in character? How do you raise consciousness of interdependence in a country like the United States that is so narrowly focused on domestic policies? A lot of the work I am doing now is an attempt to deal in a practical fashion with the questions that you can glean from the books.

Q: How important is public deliberation in a democracy? Can you imagine a form of democracy without that feature?

B: I can certainly imagine a form of democracy that doesn't depend on public deliberation because that is what we have presently in most democracies. But I think non-deliberative democracy is deeply dangerous. That is the road to tyranny of the majority, the road to mob rule, to the manipulation of public opinion.

Most critics of democracy think that most of the time democracy means manipulation and that you rarely have real deliberation. I don't agree with that 'neo-elitist critique' because I think the public capacity for deliberation is much greater than neo-elitist critics of democracy per se think it is. But I do think – and this comes back to the question on the media – deliberation needs leadership, it needs shapers and influencers. We need public officials who want public deliberation. Both Obama and Clinton, and possibly even McCain, much more than Bush, are willing to acknowledge that public deliberation is important; they want the public good to be debated. From that point of view, it has been a quite remarkable election. But the media remain the primary obstacle to a more deliberative approach to politics. They are not only not interested in deliberation, they are a serious impediment to it. Their potential role to encourage and help deliberation is defeated by sound bite television, by polarization and the quest for ratings, by the need to sell advertising. The great crisis of American democracy raises the question whether after forty years of privatization and commercialization of politics anything like public deliberation – either 'public' or 'deliberation' – really exists anymore. Part of the work of public intellectuals should be to help serve public deliberation, to encourage democratic debate, and to find ways to do it. But because we ourselves are dependent on the media to have our voices out there, it is difficult for us to do so.

In terms of modeling democracy, if America is to model anything, it should be modeling public deliberation as the indispensable prelude and foundation for viable, effective democracy. Right now, we are doing that very, very badly, and that is alarming. The hope is in the new age of Obama, even as the global economic crisis pushes democracy against the wall, deliberation and engagement may increase as government once more becomes important.

Q: Dr. Barber, thank you very much for your time.

B: You are most welcome, and thank you.

John Bolton

Former U.S. Ambassador to the United Nations
Former Under Secretary of State for Arms Control
Senior Fellow, American Enterprise Institute for Public Policy
Research, Washington, D.C.

Q: Mr. Bolton, what audience do you have in mind for your publications?

B: For this book – *Surrender Is Not An Option* –, it was the general readership. In other words, this was not a book written for academics, or specialists. There were many issues that were not covered that might have been in such a book. But it was intended, at the same time, to be very specific so that a broad audience would have a better understanding of what happens in the formulation of foreign policy, and what happens in the State Department, and the UN. For me, that was a hard line to walk because to sell to the general public is very different from selling to an academic audience. But I felt it was important to try and do that.

Q: Is there an educational aspect to what you do – to provide the public with a frame of knowledge?

B: Yes, for sure. Because I think a lot of people don't understand how policy is made in the State Department. They don't appreciate that a president doesn't come in and say "this is what I want to do," and then it happens automatically. It doesn't. That poses a problem for democratic theory. But unless you can explain that, most people just wouldn't believe it, right?

Q: You prefer "the democratic expression of opinion in free societies like ours to make policy, rather than obscure international negotiations by the High Minded." This seems to hint at an egalitarian conception of democracy.

B: The United States is different from most European countries in that policy, foreign policy, is set in a broader political context. People fight about it in congress, interest groups fight about it. It is not simply an area of discussion in the Foreign Ministry, among a small group of the political elite. A lot of people object to that, particularly at the State Department. One reason why I am talking about this here is that there are people who are dissatisfied with the outcome democratically in the United States, with gun control, for example, and they try and expand the issue to result through international treaties – which are these negotiations among the High Minded. As opposed to debating it in the United States.

Q: Why did you choose American foreign policy as the area to focus on in your book?

B: The things I talk about, gun control, abortion, death penalty, a range of issues that I would consider domestic issues are nonetheless debated in international forums, in the international fore more and more. Many Europeans want it that way. In my book, I identify what the problem with that is.

Q: How would you define the term 'public intellectual'? Does this term still point to something relevant?

B: I don't like it much as a term. I don't like the 'intellectual' part much, frankly. It covers a very broad territory. It covers people who are basically intellectuals, but who write, speak, appear on TV shows – who are more visible than if they simply stayed in the academy. But it also covers people who are engaged in politics, who wouldn't really participate in academic life. Maybe at one point, it had a sensible definition. By now, it includes almost anybody who speaks, or writes broadly, and by definition, they can't all be intellectuals.

Q: Do you find it problematic that the majority of intellectuals today are affiliated with the academy, the government, or a think tank – and still claim to act somewhat outside of purpose-driven constraints?

B: Most people would say it dates from the New Deal involvement by academics in practical politics. Some would date it back to Wilson's presidency. He was I think the first university president to be President of the United States. So it is a relatively recent phenomenon. But I have never actually studied it, I am not sure I would be the best person to comment on it.

Q: Looking at the very recent past, would you say that the authority of intellectuals has increased since September 11, 2001 – possibly due to a

demand on the side of the American public for a guiding voice of reason
that will explain to them the course of their nation?

B: I don't think so. I don't know how you would measure that kind of
trend. Whenever there is a controversial international policy, there is going to be more debate over it. In that sense, there is more people partici-
pating, more people arguing. And maybe it is more correlated with controversial policy – Vietnam, the war in Iraq – than with particular patterns
by the intellectuals themselves.

Q: Your professional career includes high-level positions in practical
politics. These days, you work at a think tank. What does your audience
expect from you? Concrete policy proposals, or rather a visionary frame
for American ideals?

B: I think it is both. Different people spend more time doing one or the
other. I don't think they are exclusive opposites, I think they are comple-
mentary. This is also a characteristic of American governance that is different from European governance. You have people go in and out of the
government – I don't mean just a few people who are parliamentarians
who become ministers or junior ministers. I mean the whole phenomenon: a couple of thousand people in every administration who are political appointees. Some people call it a 'revolving door', but you have that
possibility: When you are out, there is an opportunity to reflect on what
you have done, and then to write about policy prescriptions and larger
philosophical issues. That is just part of our natural cycle, which is very
different from the typical European government experience.

Q: You seem to choose an all-encompassing approach in your book –
despite significant controversies you have experienced with a number of
fellow political figures in the past. The subtitle reads: 'Defending Amer-
ica at the United Nations and Abroad'.

B: Titles of books are picked by the publishers. This title was picked because of the end of the opening little story where I was talking about
Goldwater's defeat, and I said: "One thing was for certain: Surrender was
not an option." But then the subtitle was also picked by the publishers
because they thought people would be interested in the broader question,
not the things that happened to me – although that obviously formed a
part of it. So I wouldn't read great significance into the title, or the subtitle – except indirectly because it is what the publisher thinks is going to

attract people. I would have called the book something else, in fact something much more boring. But if you take the publishers' judgment to be their assessment of what would interest the public, then it may reflect an interesting judgment. As for the all-encompassing approach: I think the issues that I describe are all consistent philosophically, and form a pattern, at least for me. In that sense, the structure of the book is certainly coherent.

Q: What is the balance of power like between the world of 'thinkers' – the academy, the think tanks – and the world of 'doers' – the people in everyday politics?

B: Clearly, the greatest influence is by the people who are engaged in actual political activity. Again, the American experience is substantially different from Europe in that Europe is changing.

These days, most American academics stay as academics. Because there are think tanks on the Right and the Left, people who are more inclined to be active in specific public policy issues tend to be in the think tanks so they are midway between academia and hands-on government experience. Think tanks attract people who have a foot in both camps, people who have academic capabilities and inclinations, but who are also interested in government. Their influence is hard to measure, but in part, these are people who go in and out of government, for sure.

Q: I would like to read you another quote, this time from the chapter 'Free at last: Back to the firing line': "A major conceptual problem in this war is our failure to call it what it is, which is surely not a 'global war on terrorism', however evocative that title may be. [...] When President Bush decried 'Islamofascism', a cumbersome but accurate description of the problem, the High Minded criticized him, and he backed away." This seems to suggest that the world of non-practical politics holds a certain power over its practical counterpart.

B: That's true. There is an influence. But if you are actually in the government, your influence is substantially greater. There isn't any question about that.

Q: Why do you keep deciding against academia?

B: If you are in academia, you have teaching obligations. I have lived in Washington since I got out of Law School. It is different from, say, the

Kennedy administration where everybody came down from Harvard. I have zero desire to go back to New Haven, or another university town. If you are going to be in Washington, you might as well be in a think tank as opposed to a university.

Q: How do you evaluate the importance of morality in politics? Is it the task of an authority who is somewhat above the pitfalls of practical politics to watch over moral issues?

B: I would focus less on moral issues than on philosophical issues – which have moral implications, to be sure. But if it is between philosophy and morality, and politics, I would call it moral philosophy.

The advantage of thinking about these things when you are not in government is that it helps give you a structure to assimilate a huge amount of information that flows over you when you are in the government. If you just walk in and have no particular philosophical orientation – right or left – you are going to become a creature of the bureaucracy. And that happens to a lot of people, even people you think have a philosophical inclination. It is sort of keeping your compass straight to be able to have the ability outside of government to reflect on both what happened to you in the government and issues that the government now confronts that you have no direct influence over. It is easier to be on the outside in that sense because you don't have any bureaucratic restraints. That is what I mean by 'going back on the firing line'. I don't have to clear what I say with anybody. When I was in the government, I had to clear it with what seemed like half of the bureaucracy. It is important not to self-censor when you are in the position of freedom that people like I am are in now. This is where you should express your opinions fully, and enter into the debate. For that reason, there isn't any need to compromise, self-censor, or limit the articulation of your opinions.

Q: Does the 'position of freedom' as you describe it make a critical, or somewhat more distanced view of the situation possible?

B: Absolutely. There is a saying in government that the urgent crowds out the important. That's true. Things happen that have to be addressed, whether they are your priority or not. A major part of defining what being in the government is like is keeping your priorities first. This is a real problem in the bureaucracy, and if you are not used to it you find the bureaucracy setting your priorities instead of the other way round. Being on the outside allows you to rethink your experiences, and to see whether you succeeded or failed, and if you didn't do as well as you wanted to, what you would do differently next time.

Q: Would you agree that there is a general consensus across political affiliations and party lines that the American version of democracy should be disseminated throughout the world, and that controversies arise mainly as to how that dissemination can be carried out most effectively?

B: I think there is a pretty broad consensus for that. In our current circumstances, people are attacking the perception that the overthrow of Saddam Hussein and a range of other policies were driven by a desire to spread democracy mindlessly around the world. I don't think that is the case. At the same time, when Democrats were in, Republicans criticized the Clinton administration for nation-building. I don't think those things are inconsistent. In Iraq, we made a mistake in taking control through the coalition authority. We should have given more authority back to the Iraqis. Exaggerating for effect, I would say we should have given them a copy of the Federalist Papers and said: "It's up to you now." Because we can't create a democracy in Iraq or anywhere else. We can say "we think this is the way you want to go." But they have to develop habits of political cooperation, and competition, and the values of a democracy because they think it is right for them, not because we say so.

You can't impose a democracy top-down, in the experience that America had in real occupations since World War II. Most people would argue that we were more 'successful' in Germany because there was a history, a tradition of elections and efforts to achieve a democratic society that failed when the Weimar Republic collapsed. Whereas in Japan, with much less of a history, and one that was farther back in the early 1900s, it was much harder for the people to remember what they had done before. The point is: There was a history in Germany, there was zero history in Iraq. And that's why they have to come to their own conclusion about democracy. If the Democrats were to win in November, you will not hear them say: "We don't care about democracy in Iraq." That will not happen. In some respects, the Democratic side as demonstrated during the Clinton administration was less realistic about the prospects for democracy than the Bush administration is now. But this shouldn't surprise anybody. How is anybody in the United States seriously going to argue that we want them to adopt some other form of government? Maybe they will because it is their country. But we are not going to say: "We favor an authoritarian government for Iraq."

Q: So how should the United States convey the notion that democracy is the best solution?

B: The best way to convey it is by example. I have always felt that the most effective form of foreign aid that the United States has ever given out is bringing people to the United States for educational programs: University training, professional education. We are what we are, our system is what it is. We can talk about public diplomacy and making it more understandable, but fundamentally, if people have a chance to come here, they can judge for themselves.

Some people don't like it. The fellow who helped to revive the Muslim Brotherhood in Egypt, Sayyid Qutb, came to the United States and was appalled by Greeley College in Colorado. That campus actually banned alcohol, and he still thought American society was decadent and corrupt. And Colorado is not New York, to put it that way. So people can come and get the wrong impression, they can become anti-American, they can reject capitalism and democracy. There is no guarantee to prevent that. By and large, people come and when they go home, they may not say "boy, I think America is great," but they end up promoting the same kinds of values. So it is a question of example, and people can make up their own mind when they see it in operation, with all its flaws.

Q: I would ask you to elaborate a little bit on another quote from your book: "Diplomacy should come to mean advocacy. Advocacy for American interests must be the priority, not compromise and conciliation for their own sake."

B: The problem, culturally, with the State Department is that it views stability of relationships as the highest priority. Therefore, you don't want to be too pushy, you don't want to be too strong an advocate because that might result in instability. What that means is that our interests are compromised far more often than they need to be. So when I say 'advocacy' I mean the point of having a diplomatic corps is to protect our interests and to advance them where possible, not to achieve the platonic best version of an international situation. Other countries' diplomatic services are advancing their interests, and there is nothing wrong with that. I just think ours should be more effective at advancing our interests.

Q: How important is it that the United States remains the sole super-power in the world?

B: It will evolve depending on what other countries do. That is determined in part by the underlying strength of the society. It is not a goal to be the world's only remaining superpower. It is maybe a consequence of what we do, but it shouldn't be an objective. If you were to set it as a goal, you would risk compromising internal arrangements: The individual freedom in this country, and what the product of individual choice is. That would be a mistake. And maybe the product of individual choice is that people don't want to take up the burdens of worrying about much of the rest of the world. If that is what people's free choices turn out to be, then you ought to leave it at that. I don't like the idea that 'we are the world's current imperial power, and that is a good thing, and we ought to sustain it'. We are what we are, and it will sustain itself or not, depending on what we want to do, not because that should be our objective.

Q: What is the role of the United Nations?

B: It is one instrument of foreign policy, it is not the exclusive instrument. Most Americans look at the UN the same way they look at much of life. Americans are very practical people. They don't look at it through ideological prisms, they say: "Is this something that can help us solve international problems?" If it can't, they say: "Can we fix it?" And if you can't fix it, they say: "Fine, what else is there?" And they look at a range of alternatives. There are a lot of utensils you can use for foreign policy, and the United Nations is kind of like a butter knife. There is nothing wrong with a butter knife. But you need to understand it is not a steak knife, it is not a fork. It is something that can be useful, but not uniformly, not inevitably, not in every context.

Q: What is the "steak knife" in this context?

B: Fundamentally, it is the United States, and the force that we have available to us, and that very few other countries have or are willing to project. A lot of other countries have strong militaries, but very few can project force around the world. From our point of view, that is unfortunate because it means we end up carrying most of the burden.

Q: My last set of questions deals with the issue of public deliberation in American democracy. Can you imagine a form of democracy without that feature?

B: It would be almost impossible to imagine that. Our history from the beginning reflects it. People came to Jamestown in 1607, and the first thing they did was form a government. Pilgrims come to Plymouth Rock in 1620, and they sign the Mayflower Compact. It is all part of the discussions, the traditional town meetings in New England, and so on. Large part of the reason why the original settlers came here was that they wanted to get away from the environment that they faced in England and other places. It has been a development from the outset that has required extensive public discussion, and I just don't see that changing.

Q: What's your role in this – as a leading figure of the political class, as the author of a book like Surrender Is Not An Option?

B: I wanted to tell the story of what I thought we did right or wrong in the Bush administration. It is important to understand what actually happened, not what the sometimes distorted press accounts of it would be. So that people can then draw their own conclusions about what you do the next time to avoid the mistakes that we made, and hopefully to build on things we did right.

So I view this as part of the public debate in this country – also in relation with the election campaign – but also as something written for historical purposes. I have a lot of very specific descriptions of things that happened. A lot of people may not agree with my conclusions, but if they want to disagree, they have to rebut the facts. They have to have an alternative narrative that provides support for whatever conclusions they want to come to. I felt it was important to get these facts out on the public market.

Q: You emphasize the importance of practical political action, and yet you also publish a voluminous book with an elaborate conceptual framework...

B: You need both. You have to have the philosophical framework, but then you have to be able to show how to get things done. Especially with the American Conservatives, they don't like to be in the government in the first place. It is easy to talk about the theory, and not be able to accomplish the practical things. For those who think the theory is abstract –

that is a prescription to get lost in the bureaucracy, lost in the maze, and not accomplish anything, either. You can fail for a lot of different reasons. The best way to avoid that is to carry the philosophical framework with you, but to understand – which is what I try to explain in the book – how to maneuver within the system that you have got, whether you like it or not. Otherwise you are not going to get your policies and your philosophy implemented.

Q: Why don't Conservatives like to be in the government?

B: It is very bureaucratic, and very frustrating. And very different from private enterprise where there is a premium on accomplishing something. But even in the US government, people would look at the UN as a place where there is even less interest in getting things done, where the process and the stability of the process has its own independent value – for many people a higher value than actually getting something done. Trying to describe all that was another aspect that I was after.

Q: Mr. Bolton, thanks very much for your time.

B: Thank you.

Zbigniew Brzezinski

Former National Security Advisor
Robert E. Osgood Professor of American foreign policy,
School of Advanced International Studies, Johns Hopkins
University, Washington, D.C.

Q: Dr. Brzezinski, what audience do you have in mind for your publications?

B: The internationally minded, educated portions of American society. Not just academics – certainly, it includes academics and students – but also that part of American society which either through business activities, or work in the government, or political involvement, is in some fashion engaged in shaping, directly or indirectly, American policy.

Q: Is there an 'education project' involved in what you do?

B: Yes, absolutely. Ultimately, America is a democracy. The intelligent portions of American society, if enlightened and engaged, can help to shape a more responsive, more historically meaningful American policy toward the world. Ignorance makes many Americans susceptible to simple-minded demagogy.

Q: Given the fact that American foreign policy is a rather complex affair, who is going to bridge the gap between what is going on at the governmental level, and what the public should know about and understand? In other words: Is this sort of translation work the main purpose of a book like The Choice?

B: Yes, in a sense. Obviously, I anticipate that there will be several different audiences for this book. Hopefully some leading political figures – including perhaps even some that are competing for the presidency – will have read it, and will have assimilated some of its notions and ideas. And that it will be read by others who might assimilate some portions of it. And that it will also influence the younger, future elite of this country.

Q: Your professional background spans high-level positions in both the government and the academy. What does your audience expect from you: concrete policy proposals, or rather a visionary framework for American ideals?

B: I don't know. I write the book that I feel like writing. I don't try to gauge what might be the expectations of different groups. When I write a book like this, I say what is on my mind, and how I think the issues should be defined or answered.

Q: In your conclusion, you talk about "a compelling vision of a global community" in relation with America's role in the world. For all the positions you held in practical politics, there still seems to be a need for a visionary frame – would you agree?

B: Yes, I think so.

Q: What is the balance of power like between the 'doers' of practical politics and the 'thinkers' of academia?

B: You can't measure that. It really depends on how different individuals are guided by such notions. I wouldn't even know how to answer it in respect to myself.

Q: Speaking from your position as a practical politician, what can the academic world add to what you do?

B: I don't think the academic world can add that much, actually, to be perfectly frank. The tendency of academics is to emphasize very systematic parsing and analysis rather than vision and action.

Q: Why did you decide to trade a position in practical politics for one in the academic world?

B: I didn't have any choice. You either are in power, or you can influence power. Or you can be doing something entirely different.

Q: Influencing power is the motivation for your work?

B: Yes, of course. I believe that ideas translated into practice can shape reality. Power is not an end in itself, as far as I am concerned. Power is a means to an end. You can exercise power directly, or you can exercise power indirectly.

Q: Has the authority of public intellectuals increased since September 11? Perhaps because the American public is in search of orientation with regard to the course of their nation?

B: For some, it has gone down. For some, it has gone up.

Q: Which are the ones it has gone up for?

B: The critics.

Q: Why is this?

B: Because of what has happened after the attack on Iraq.

Q: So Iraq is another turning point, following the previous one in 2001?

B: I don't think 2001 was such a turning point. I think the reaction to 2001 which surfaced in 2003 discredited those who are commonly called Neocons, and has shifted public influence to those who are critical of the nature of that response.

Q: Dr. Brzezinski, thanks a lot for your time.

B: Good to talk to you.

Noam Chomsky

Institute Professor and Professor of Linguistics Emeritus,
Massachusetts Institute of Technology (MIT), Boston, MA

Q: Professor Chomsky, September 11 and its aftermath seem to have re-invigorated the public intellectual debate on the course of American for-eign policy...

C: Actually, I don't really agree that there is much of a debate because the country, especially the educated classes, are so deeply indoctrinated that they can't have a debate. It is kind of like the old Soviet Union: There couldn't be a debate in the old Soviet Union about 'is it right or wrong to invade Afghanistan' because the question doesn't arise. If the Russians want to do it, it is right.

And it is the same here. There is no debate about Iraq. Within the educated sectors, there is literally no principled objection to invading another country. By 'principled objection' I mean the kind of objection we would have when the Russians invade Afghanistan, or when Saddam Hussein invades Kuwait. We don't say of the invasions that they were 'strategic blunders' – Barack Obama about Iraq – and we don't say that the Russians or Saddam got into a civil war that they can't win – Clinton. That is as far as you can go in the United States. So there is no debate. Everyone rigidly keeps to the party line. If we do it, it is legitimate. The only question you can raise is: Is it costing us too much? That is why the debate over Iraq – such as it is – has declined. As American casualties go down, you can't talk about it.

I read a front page story in the *New York Times* this morning about how the Democrats are going to deal with Iraq in the campaign. What they are going to do is play up the economic costs. You go back to, say, Nazi-Germany after Stalingrad, there were Nazi generals who thought it was just costing too much, a two-front war was a stupid blunder. That is like left-wing American intellectuals: Strategic blunder, bad mistake. It was the same with Vietnam. There were tons of discussion of Vietnam, but the farthest you could go was someone like Anthony Lewis – way out of the left extreme – who at the end of the war said: "The war began with blundering efforts to do good." 'Efforts to do good' is a tautology. Our state did it, so it is efforts to do good – that is tautologous. 'Blundering' means it didn't work out too well. So the first sentence is a virtual tautology. Then he said: "By 1969" – this is an interesting year, it is a year and a half after the business world turned against the war – "it was clear that we could not achieve our goal of a democratic Vietnam at costs acceptable to ourselves." Notice that the only problem was that the costs were getting too high to *us*. But if you are an intellectual, you have to believe. 1975, when Lewis wrote this in retrospect, is an interesting year because in that year the first polls were taken about what the public thought about Vietnam. Seventy percent said it is "not a mistake," it is "fundamentally wrong and immoral." That is the public, and they don't have any role in political decisions in our system, they are a margin. But among intellectuals, I don't think there is a debate, except at the margins.

Q: What about publications on American foreign policy? The authors seem to deal with the issue in a deliberately accessible way, reaching out to a large readership.

C: They deal with the issue because they are living in the home of the Godfather. Actually, a lot of these people are trying to get a job in the next administration. It is almost comical. You see it in places like Harvard and MIT: They are putting themselves forward – "Can I be in the next administration?" It really started with the Kennedy intellectuals. Then people got the idea and thought "well look, if Walt Rostow can do it, I can do it. If Kissinger can do it, I can do it." Before every election, particular people present themselves as having big thoughts about how to run the world. But I don't call that a debate. This is like a debate within the German general staff after Stalingrad. There were also debates, and maybe they were among intellectuals. I don't know Germany well enough, but I wouldn't be surprised.

Q: What is the main reason for you to publish a book like Hegemony or Survival*; what audience do you have in mind?*

C: I am not talking to intellectuals. It is like talking to members of the Communist Party. I am talking to the public. And the public has an influence. The intellectual classes don't like it, they don't want them to have an influence, but they do. It is a very free society. Let me make it concrete: When seventy percent of the American population agreed in 1975 that the war was fundamentally wrong and immoral, and not a mistake, it was not because of what I said. It is because a lot of people were saying that and acting on it, and it spread among the public, especially young people.

Q: So it spreads on its own? It doesn't take someone to put forward an 'educational project' for the public? Some kind of 'public schooling'?

C: Taking the term literally, you can't get into the schools. By now actually you can, to an extent. The country is a lot more civilized than it was in the 1960s, thanks to the sixties activism. Take my friend Howard Zinn. When his book *A People's History of the United States* came out, it was just anathema. It is still anathema among educated circles. But high school students read it. In fact, some of it is even assigned. It is just because the society over time gets more civilized. Intellectuals are usually left behind. But they sort of follow along at some distance. I think that is generally true. It is true through history. The educated classes are usually more indoctrinated, more subordinate to power, less capable of thinking for themselves than the general public. There is even political science evidence on this.

Q: What does the term 'public intellectual' mean for you?

C: It means usually subordination to power. It is somebody who is no different from anyone else, except that they have the degree of privilege, the resources, and the level of subordination to power which enable them to enter into articulate discourse. People like me are on the fringe. You do get invited once every two years or so to be on NPR, but you are on the fringe. There is an entry requirement: You have to be sufficiently subordinate to power. For example, take Iraq or Vietnam, if you say we should apply to ourselves the same principles we apply to others, you are out of the debate. If anyone were to say "invading Iraq is like what the Nazi war criminals were hanged for" – which happens to be correct – you are out of the debate because some truths are not allowed. You have to say "it was blundering efforts to do good." In fact, you say that in the face of the most awesome counter-evidence.

Take a look at the notion of democracy promotion which is supposed to be our goal. I have run through the scholarly and general literature on democracy promotion – virtually every article, the roots of the Bush doctrine or whatever, is on democracy promotion. Now look at history. When we invaded Iraq, there was almost no mention of democracy promotion, just a little bit on the side: With anything you do, you say we want democracy to spread. It had nothing to do with it. Right at that time, Donald Rumsfeld made an interesting distinction – which has stuck – between 'Old Europe' and 'New Europe'. There is a very sharp criterion distinguishing them: 'Old Europe' is the bad guys, where the government went along with a large majority of the population. 'New Europe', the good guys, is where the government violated the opinions of an even larger majority of the population. Aznar was the super-good guy, he was even invited to the Azores summit meeting. He had the support of two percent of the population, but he was the good guy. That alone shows such hatred of democracy that it is almost indescribable, but nobody can see it. So you start by demonstrating your hatred for democracy, then you go to war. There is almost no talk about democracy. Then they fail to find weapons of mass destruction. They have got a problem, so they need some new pretext. In November, eight months after the invasion, Bush makes a speech at the National Endowment for Democracy, very wide coverage, a lot of publicity, saying our goal is to create democracy in the Middle East and the world. Intellectuals fall over themselves in awe about how marvelous we are: We want to spread democracy in the world, and that is why we invaded Iraq. You couldn't do better in the old Communist Party – it is laughable. And then, event after event, systematically, they oppose democracy.

There has been one free election in the Arab world, in January 2006. It was monitored, and everybody said it was free and fair: Palestine. The wrong guys won. Instantly, the United States turned to punishing the population harshly for voting the wrong way in a free election. Nobody sees any contradiction there. We love democracy, we are promoting democracy, but you better vote the right way, or we will crush you. That is promoting democracy.

You can go through the rest of the story, it is all the same. In fact, it is even understood in scholarship. If you read one of the leading scholar activists involved in democracy promotion, Thomas Carothers, who has written books on the subject – he is all in favor of it, but he is a good scholar – he says that if you look at the record, you see something very strange. Every American president has been "schizophrenic." On the one hand, they love democracy. On the other hand, they undermine democracy unless it conforms to US strategic and economic objectives. It is like some psychiatric disorder, they are all suffering from schizophrenia. Do we say that when we talk about Stalin? He loved democracy, too. He was defending the peoples' democracies from the Fascists. Do we say he was schizophrenic? No. Maybe he believed his own craziness. You can believe your craziness, too. But it was just a cover for what you are actually doing. We take that for granted when we study enemies. With ourselves, we cannot do it. If the leader says something, it is true. You can't question it. That level of indoctrination goes right through history. It is very rare to find intellectuals who are critical of power. They claim otherwise. But take a careful look.

Q: The subordination of the intellectual elite to the power elite – your ranking is clear. Whose task is it to watch over moral issues in politics, though? Is it up to an authority like the intellectuals who at least claim to act somewhat from outside the fray of everyday politics?

C: It is the task of every human being. And those people like me, who happen to be very privileged – college professor, resources, training, and everything – have an extra responsibility. That is a moral principle. Everyone has the responsibility to ensure to the extent that they can that the acts they participate in are the right ones. You are responsible for the anticipated consequences of your actions, that is true if you are a college professor or a janitor. However, the degree of responsibility varies with privilege. I have got a lot more responsibility than the guy who cleans the room because he can't do much. He doesn't have the privilege that I have. That is just elementary morality. That is nothing to talk about.

Q: You chose as your way of living up to that responsibility to become an academic. Why?

C: I chose the academic world because I am excited by the intellectual challenge. Actually, I didn't choose the academic world. I am here by accident. I have almost no credentials – which is why I am teaching at MIT, not at Harvard, or Princeton. Later, I could have got a job at the Ivy League, but at the beginning, I had no credentials.

MIT is a science university, they don't give a damn about credentials, they care whether your work is interesting. So I was working in an electronics lab and went off from there. Linguistics altogether generally developed outside the major academic centers because it was breaking with tradition. The academic centers tend to be conservative and traditional. That is true all over Europe – very hard to break in. Here it started at MIT, not at Harvard. As a matter of fact, the Ivy League universities were some of the latest and last ones to allow it in, and it has been replicated throughout Europe and Japan. The academic professions – except for the natural sciences which are pretty open and free – are very rigid. You have to have a guild, you have to protect yourself. That is why there is a distinction made between the experts in policy and the rest of us. The fact of the matter is, there are no experts in policy. To be an expert in policy, you have to be literate. That is the only requirement. You have to learn a couple of things about statistics, maybe. But beyond that, it is within the grasp of any high school student. They have to pretend otherwise, though, because you have to protect yourself. It is striking, I have seen it in my career. My own work has ranged from mathematics to political issues. I don't have any training in any of it. I am self-educated. If I give a talk at the Harvard Graduate Seminar on mathematics, nobody would ever ask "what are your credentials, where did you do your Ph.D.?" If anybody said something like that, they would be ridiculed. They want to know what you are saying. On the rare occasions when I could talk at a political science department, there would be all kinds of little jokes like "I don't talk about linguistics, how can you talk about political science?" Generally, the less substance there is to a field, the more people have to protect themselves. Not surprising.

Q: There is a large number of people who want to listen to what you have to say, though. Has that number increased since the 9/11 terror attacks? In other words: Is there a demand on the side of the public for a guiding voice of reason that will explain to them the course of their nation?

C: When I started giving talks on the Vietnam War, I would talk in somebody's living room, or in a church with four people. Over the years, things changed. There is a reason why the 1960s are so hated by intellectuals. They are called the 'times of trouble'. The reason is the country was getting more civilized. And that is intolerable. It was happening all other the world. What they like is a couple of crazies on the fringes, that's where it gets played up. What was really happening was that the Western world was getting more civilized, in all sorts of ways: Women's rights, ecological concerns, minority rights, opposition to oppression. That is civilization: Becoming more democratic.

The Crisis of Democracy is a book which was published by the Trilateral Commission – liberal internationalists in the US, Europe, and Japan – in the early 1970s. It is a book of concern about the increase of democracy that was coming about in the 1960s, which is why it says 'crisis'. They put it in jargon, saying there is too much pressure on the state, the state can't answer all these demands. What they are really saying, though, is that people who are supposed to be passive and acquiescent – like women, and the youth, and workers, and farmers – are getting into the political arena, pushing their demand. The state is only supposed to respond to the demands of business – they don't say this, it is the hidden premise. They say we have to have more moderation in democracy. Since they were talking to each other, it was pretty frank. They were concerned about what they called the institutions "responsible for the indoctrination of the young." Namely, the schools, the colleges, the churches, they were not indoctrinating the young properly, they would have to become more harsh, or the state would have to come in and force things. These were liberal internationalists, not the right wing. They were terrified by the increase in democracy. We have been in a period ever since where they have been trying to crush it – but it hasn't really worked.

Q: What about this idea of moderation in democracy you mentioned? Is it any different today from the time before 2001, and if so, in what way?

C: There are some interesting differences. Take the top domestic concern for Americans – it has been the major issue for decades: The health care system, which is a complete catastrophe. Twice the per capita costs of other industrial countries and some of the worst outcomes. If you are not an ideological fanatic, you know the reason: It is the only privatized system. A catastrophe, and people know it. A large majority want a single-payer system, a kind of national health care, like Medicare. Up until the year 2004, in elections that was unmentionable. If you look back at 2004, the press said that candidates can't mention government involved in the health care system because it "lacks political support." The pharmaceutical industry is opposed, the financial institutions are opposed, so no need to even mention it. This year, for the first time, it is mentioned. In fact, the Democrats have programs which are moving in that direction.

What changed between 2004 and 2008? Not public opinion, it is the same. But something did change. A segment of the manufacturing industry is becoming concerned about the abysmal health care system: It is costing them too much. And when a segment of concentrated capital becomes concerned about something, it becomes politically possible. Honest commentators and political scientists in the United States would tell you what this means. It is not a deep secret. It is the only thing that has changed in the last four years. And what it tells you is: It is the way the country is run. You might think the political scientists don't know it. But the public does. This year's polls on people's attitudes toward democracy just came out: 80% of the public says that the country is run by a few big interests looking out for themselves, not for the benefit of the people. Do you find that in the political science literature? If you look at the footnotes, you can, actually. But that is what the public thinks, and they are largely right.

Now public intellectuals, their responsibility is to suppress all this. For example, the media don't report these polls. Systematically. Actually, it is quite striking this time because there was a series of polls on democracy, and in one of them was a question about oppression in Tibet. Of all the collection of polls, that was the only one that was reported because we are allowed to talk about the bad things that other people do. The degree of subordination to power is pretty astonishing.

Q: You mention health care as a domestic issue. What about foreign policy issues?

C: Same thing. Take the biggest issue that is coming up: Iran. US public opinion has been carefully studied. It happens to be the same as Iranian public opinion, which is also studied. A large majority of the public – by 3:1 – is opposed to any threats. *Any threats.* They say "let's just have negotiations, and diplomatic relations." Roughly the same percentage – 75% – say that Iran has a right to have nuclear power, but not nuclear weapons. The same percentage say we should institute a nuclear weapons free zone in the Middle East – Iran is to be treated like everybody else. That happens to be Iran's position, and has been for years. But nobody knows that because you don't get a report. Can you imagine a candidate saying this? Or a commentator writing it? In fact the press refused to publish the polls – which were from the major polling agency in the world, the Program on International Policy Attitudes at the University of Maryland. They were not reported. And that is systematic. If the country was democratic, this problem would be resolved.

It is the same with Cuba: For about thirty years, a large majority of the public wants to enter into normal diplomatic relations with Cuba. It can't be reported. No candidate can say it. No political commentator can say it. The opinion of the public, which on many issues is quite sane, is scarcely reported. And this has been studied, by some political scientists as well.

Q: Would you say that, although you point out these things, there is no chance for an intellectual debate to develop because your peers are not willing to pick up on them?

C: There is no serious debate among the group that you are talking about – the 'acceptable' public intellectuals. The ones who write articles, are on television, testify at the Center on Foreign Relations Committee. Among them, there is essentially no debate. Maybe not none at all. It is still not a totalitarian system, it is a free society.

Q: Is there no debate because there is a general consensus – reaching across political affiliations and party boundaries – that the United States should remain the sole superpower in the world? And that the American version of democracy should be spread throughout the world?

C: Do we *want* to spread the American version of democracy? I just gave a talk on Latin America and pointed out that if you want a model of democracy, you don't want to look at the United States where people barely participate – and know it. You want to look at the poorest country in South America, namely Bolivia. They had a real free election in which the mass of the population participated actively. They elected someone from their own ranks, they entered into the issues, they had been engaged in these issues for years, not just pushing a button on Election Day. That is democracy. So if you want democracy, turn to Bolivia, not to the United States where 80% of the population recognize that the government has nothing to do with them. If anybody is interested in democracy promotion, they should take lessons from Bolivia. Try to say that publicly. People are confused, or outraged. Unless I talk to a general audience – they understand it very quickly.

Q: So the ones who could intervene, who could speak up from an influential position, they are the ones too closely affiliated with power to do so?

C: George Orwell wrote about this – in a suppressed essay. You probably read *Animal Farm*. But you didn't read the introduction to *Animal Farm*, I am pretty sure. The introduction wasn't published, it was found in his unpublished papers thirty years later. It is not one of his greatest essays,

but it is worth looking at it. He says that there are a lot of books and articles about the totalitarian monster we all hate. But in free England, it is
not much different. In England, unpopular ideas can be suppressed without the use of force, partly because the press is owned by wealthy men
who have every reason not to want certain ideas to be spread. But the
more important reason is that if you are well educated, cultured, you just
have it instilled into you that there are certain things that "it wouldn't do
to say." It is part of your nature. You can't even think the thoughts. You
can't think the thought that the United States is *not* trying to do good.
That it is like every other power in the world. You can't think the thought
that 80% of the population believe that the country is run by a few big
interests looking after themselves. But if you are well-educated, you just
can't think that anymore. Education is largely a process of indoctrination.
The institutions are responsible for the indoctrination of the young, and
by and large, they work. Not completely. That is why you get student activism and things like that.

*Q: How should the United States convey its position on the world stage to
other nations?*

C: What is their position, first of all? Is it the position of the population,
or the elite position? Take Iran. Is it the position of the population? That
is what I think should be articulated here and in the world. But it is not
the position of educated people, of public intellectuals, of candidates, of
newspapers, and so on. And it is the same with a lot of other issues, including domestic issues. So it doesn't make sense to ask: How should the
US convey its position? Which US are you talking about – the large majority of the population, or the people that make up university faculties?
That's a different world.

*Q: Who is going to bridge that gap? Is there a chance to achieve this at
all?*

C: Sure. That's why we have the freedom that we have. Take, say, freedom of speech, maybe one of the most important things. The United
States happens to be in the lead in the world on the freedom of speech,
way beyond Europe. In Europe, freedom of speech is sharply limited in
various ways. But in the United States, it is protected. Where did that
come from? It is not in the Bill of Rights. These things are determined by
court decisions. Freedom of speech issues didn't reach the Supreme Court

until the 20th century. And then they began to be supported in dissents. The first strong court decision in favor of freedom of speech – striking down seditious libel, which is still upheld outside the United States, as far as I know – was in the course of the Civil Rights Movement, in a case involving Martin Luther King. You have a large, engaged, popular movement, you get progress. You can go through the rest of the freedoms we have, and it is the same. Europe is backward in this respect, European intellectuals particularly. They don't even get upset when France, for example, has laws saying that if the Holy State determines that something is a historical truth, you can be sentenced and punished if you don't go along. That is a law which they apply.

Q: Professor Chomsky, thank you very much for your time.

C: You are welcome.

Jean Bethke Elshtain

Laura Spelman Rockefeller Professor of Social and Political
Ethics
University of Chicago Divinity School, IL
Contributing Editor, *The New Republic*

Q: Professor Elshtain, what audience do you have in mind for your publications?

E: In order to answer that I have to say a few words about my general understanding – and it is not unique to me – of the role of intellectuals in a democratic society.

One assumes, whether rightly or wrongly, a reasonably well educated group – still a minority of any total population – that is also interested in political issues on a more or less continuing basis. Most people become interested just as an election approaches. The audience I imagine is an audience that tries to keep up with public debates, that cares about what is happening in the world, and what America is doing in the world, and what America's role in the world is or should be. One assumes most likely a college-educated audience, and people who are committed to some notion of a public arena or public discourse, a way to engage and a way to debate. It is possible that this is a kind of idealized version of being public, but if someone is frustrated as I have been for my entire academic life with the narrowly specialized kinds of discussions one often gets in the academy, then if you want to avoid doing that, if you are going to write anything at all, you clearly have to imagine an audience that is not just the audience of academic international relations thinkers, for example. Or in the case of the just war tradition, moral theologians.

That is the kind of audience I imagine, whether rightly or wrongly. This also determines how you write if you want your writing to be accessible. You want to footnote texts or articles that other people can read – they don't have to go to an archive somewhere, it is pretty readily available – so that they can decide, if they want to pursue the question further, that you have either made a decent case or not, or that you have used the sources well. So there is also an aspect of accountability to this – you have to be held accountable by this wider imagined group of people. Of course it is hard to determine how well you have done. The book review is another type of story. Books are often handed to experts, actually. But you can kind of tell you are reaching people given the letters you receive, emails you receive – a lot of them are people who are angry with you, but you also get lots of letters from folks who are supportive, or who have read *Just War Against Terror* and say "I think this is compelling, but that is not so compelling." That tells me that they are reading pretty carefully, carefully enough to make certain discernments. The letters that have meant the most to me have been the ones I received from soldiers. They had read the book and they said they were glad that someone in the academy recognized that they tried their best with their rules of engagement to fight fairly and to not endanger civilians. They are confronted with some very nasty stuff about what it is they do – and especially what it is that American soldiers do – that they find terribly unfair. For the last thirty-five to forty years, I have always published in places that were not typically scholarly as well as in scholarly outlets. I have always imagined a somewhat wider audience than the academy itself.

Q: Is there an issue of 'public schooling' involved in what you do – an education project for the American public?

E: Yes. There is a kind of schooling or educational process involved here in trying to offer people a way to think about some of the exigent issues that confront American society – not American society exclusively –, and what are maybe some helpful categories to think about this.

In a democratic society, education is never just the formal education that ones receives. It goes on throughout one's life. 9/11 created what might be called a very 'teachable' moment. How do you carve out some positions? It is not just seeking revenge, and anger, and "let's go get them." But it is also not being passive in light of what happened. I suppose that if one is a teacher as I am, you always imagine students. They are adult students, and you have to imagine them – as I do – as intelligent people, but you are putting yourself in a position of being a teacher in a certain sense. Fair enough.

Q: You mentioned September 11 as a 'teachable moment'. Has this led to an increased authority of American intellectuals within the public, as opposed to the common assumption of their gradual decline?

E: This is a good question. It is a hard call to say, though, whether the influence of certain people who have a public voice and make pronouncements has increased or become more prominent. I express in my book a lot of frustration at many academic intellectuals after 9/11 as they just fell into lockstep with one another. There was an automatic response that seemed to me not to be faithful to the occasion, that is not to take it as an occasion for rethinking some things. That might mean reaffirming the position you already held, it might involve altering a view that you held. But there didn't seem to be a whole lot of thought involved in it.

I suspect those whose voices were entirely predictable lost influence a bit after 9/11 because you could say "well, it's the same old thing – the world has changed, the situation has changed, but they haven't changed." Perhaps those who acknowledged, as I did, that this was a real jolt, it was shocking, and that it really called into question some of the thoughts that you had, for example, that the United States was pretty much invulnerable, gained.

Those kinds of moments open you up to further reflection. Whether the influence of those who engaged in this further reflecting has correlatively increased, that is a hard call. Certainly there was a very angry piece by Tony Judt in the *London Review of Books* where he attacked myself, Michael Walzer, and Paul Berman, and a whole lot of folks, accusing us of just providing a kind of liberal cover for reactionary politics of the Bush administration. He in fact used the old Marxist term 'useful idiots'. It was a very nasty piece to say the least. What he seemed to lament was what he perceived as our influence – "these people have too much influence." It was never my impression that I was highly influential. I do know there are people out there who read my stuff. But the idea that we were just working lockstep with the administration on things is ridiculous. I have never had as one of my ambitions being completely inside the corridors of power. You want to be able to engage power, but you don't want to be at one with it.

Perhaps from an essay like that one can say that some public voices have achieved a certain level where they are regarded at least by some as a bit authoritative. That criticism on Judt's part, however, was an exaggerated notion of the influence of public intellectuals. He is assuming that those of us who are put in that category from time to time have more influence than we actually do. But I don't know how to empirically test that. And influential with whom? You would have to look at people who actually hold power and ask "do you pay any attention to those writers, have they influenced you in any way?"

As far as the general public, I suspect that what drives the views that people hold is probably so deep that it would be difficult for any one thinker or one book or even a collection of thinkers and books to alter that substantially most of the time. I do hear from people who say "you changed my mind on this," or "you helped me to clarify my thoughts on this," or "what you say is what I believe, but I just hadn't put it in words yet." You do get those kinds of letters from time to time, which is nice because – to go back to the image of the teacher – you think maybe I have been doing an okay job if it helps people to do that. Not necessarily to absolutely agree with me, but to help them organize their thoughts in a way they hadn't done before.

Q: What in turn is the balance of power like between the world of thinkers and the world of 'hands-on' politicians? To quote from your book: "Responsible public authorities are always compelled to act in a kind of fog. As with waging war, the most certain thing about governing is its uncertainty. It is the armchair critics commenting from the sidelines who think the choices are absolutely clear."

E: The balance of power is entirely lopsided in favor of those who actually hold governmental authority. There have been periods of time in American history when academics, and intellectuals, and experts were flooding into Washington all the time, and they played an important role in certain administrations. There was a joke at the time of the Kennedy administration that all these Harvard professors spent most of their time on the shuttle flight from Boston to Washington. And you even had the court historian with Arthur Schlesinger, Jr. who was there, almost the classic way of the flattering historian – the figure wandering around, following the prince, and saying wonderful things about him.

To the extent that some intellectuals attached themselves to an administration, obviously they garner some of the authority that goes along with being that close to the corridors of power. There are reasons for why people in positions of authority – whether Democrats or Republicans – often don't take very seriously what it is a lot of academics have to say.

The reason is that so many of the comments made by academics, especially about war/peace questions, are so terribly naïve. There is just no real sense of what the limited options are. The options are not infinite. There is no sense of the limits and constraints under which these people are working. There is often an exaggerated sense of the power of the American president who 'can do whatever he wants to do' – which is simply not true. There are so many constraints that no president could just make things go according to his will. So there is a kind of "what are these people talking about?" There are some academics whose views in international relations are paid more attention to, in part because in the past they have called certain things correctly. They have really taken cognizance of the problem, they assessed what the possibilities were, and they did it in a way that was pretty clear and pretty cogent. Such people will have some greater access to those in positions of power than others seen as "whatever they say is rather beside the point."

But it is only those academics who are being consulted on a regular basis by those in power who have some of the authority and influence that goes along with that. To the extent that the rest of us have any authority, it follows from what you have to say and how you say it that may have some cogency and compelling force. So it would be more like the authority that comes with being a teacher than the authority that comes with being a power player. I don't think academics for the most part have all that much power. People in economics might be something of an exception. There are plenty of academic experts in economics – Milton Friedman would be a classic case here – who fundamentally altered how governments do business. But that is a pretty rare thing.

Q: From the beginning, American intellectuals seem to have lived with a tension: On the one hand, a need for autonomy in order to maintain a distanced perspective, on the other hand, a desire to intervene in society. What do you make of this claim to act autonomously given the fact that the majority of intellectuals today are affiliated with the government, academia, or one of the numerous think tanks?

E: This is a classic dilemma. It is a dilemma for those intellectuals who want to remain truly independent in the sense that there is a level of autonomy that they cherish, and they don't want to simply be predictable players in some scenario that is not their own. A classic example of this is Albert Camus who clearly cherished his position as a solitary thinker, but

at the same time – out of matters of conscience – could not stay away
from, could not just absent himself from the public dramas of his day.
And with his various interventions, he clearly wanted to influence the
course of politics and action. He experienced that tension you describe in
a personally very painful way.

You have to get close enough to power and authority to make a difference in how things work, but if you get too close you lose that which you
cherish so much, which is your independent voice.

I don't know how to resolve that. I think that you just live with that
tension. You are on that line between, on the one hand, "I don't want to
just be some kind of isolated crank devising manifestos that nobody cares
about and that don't seem to connect to the dilemmas that we face this
very moment." And, on the other hand, you don't want to tilt the other
direction and simply become a kind of 'house intellectual' for any particular group or administration or lobbying entity. I don't know any other
way to deal with that other than to live with the tension, and to recognize
that it is there. So you are constantly going back and forth, a little closer
here, but then step back there. Some might say this is just an attempt to
retain some kind of purity, or assumption of purity that you should just
drop, just get rid of because when you are dealing with the real world
stuff, you are always going to dirty your hands. There is great truth to
that. But I think it is one thing to know that various interventions are not
going to be just neat, tidy things – well and good. I have nothing against
people who make that decision. But if that is not the course you want to
take, then you have to be very careful that you are not going to go from
messing about in the real world to becoming a spokesperson where you
have to simply repeat and promote the views of a group of very powerful
people. For example, I have never wanted to be an advisor to a campaign,
or in a cabinet. I have nothing against the people I know who have done
that, and whom I respect very much. But there was something in me that
said "no, don't take that step."

Q: Is this the reason why you chose the position of an academic?

E: I suspect it probably is. Because you have a base to operate from. It is
a base that can become very precious, and very narrow, and very
cramped, and everybody walks in step with everybody else, and that is
the downside of it. But the upside is the fact that you do have an independent base to work from – if you choose to take advantage of it and to

use it for that purpose. Most of us who are public intellectuals have been tempted all our lives by politics, by a desire to be involved in politics, but have also had a hunch that something would happen that one wouldn't like if one became totally immersed in it.

I bet if we could get many of the folks who write about politics but are not in it *per se* to talk about their lives, you would see that coming up: Paying attention to politics all the time, a real interest in it, wondering what you would be like, what kind of candidate or office-holder you would be, but also having made choices along the way that guarantee that that is not what you are going to be doing. We see that in any campaign: It would drive me crazy to have to pander, and to repeat myself constantly, and to reduce messages. I couldn't do it.

Q: What do you think your audience expects of you? Are you expected to come forward with concrete policy proposals, or rather provide a visionary framework of American ideals?

E: People who are somewhat familiar with my work realize that I am not a public policy person as such. I always try to stay on terra firma, and to be as concrete as possible in what I am talking about. I don't want to be in some abstract philosophical arena. But I think what they are looking for primarily is the articulation of a position that has a strong ethical dimension, and that is also a position that one could reasonably endorse as being faithful to the best aspects of American society – how Americans have historically understood themselves at their best. That is why for me, in war, the notion of "bring all your force to bear, destroy them as quickly as you can" – it is just not America at her best.

Americans historically have a tension in their conscience about power, and our exercise of power in the world arena – finding it necessary, but also the tendency has been "go in, do something that you have to do, but then just get out of there as quickly as you can." There is something about being an empire, being a superpower that rests uneasily on many heads, in part because of our own history, of having been colonials, and having broken away from an empire. One has to acknowledge that dimension as well, and yet there has always been this strong moral imperative at work both in American domestic and international politics. The question is, how do you understand that moral imperative? Because that, too, has to be limited and constrained so it doesn't become a crusading mentality. That would be what people would be looking for me to articulate. To find a way to think about how to deal with really awful stuff, and yet not betray the American tradition at its best when you are doing so. I try to stay consistent with that tradition but to acknowledge the dangerous exigencies of the current moment, and to figure out how to respond to those.

Q: How do you evaluate the discussion of moral dimensions of politics? Is it the task of an authority somewhat outside the corridors of power to be mindful of morality?

E: That moral voice – there are some who denounce it in its entirety, saying that this moral voice is always dangerous, it is always narrowly moralistic, it is impositional, it should be avoided. There are others who see it as just hypocritical, as a cover-up, and what is going on underneath is power politics.

I think neither of those views is correct. The articulation of the American republic as a moral project has been so clear and so powerful throughout our history. Lincoln was brilliant in his writings about this aspect of American life, and the American experience, and the American hope. In an age that is cynical, where a lot of the traditional moral groundings of human life have given way, how do you continue to articulate that moral dimension in a way that isn't narrow, that is not prejudicial toward people who may have a different set of moral understandings?

America is different from lots of other places. One of the ways it is different is that the American republic was seen within this moral framework from the very beginning. Historically, people within the country who were dissenters because of ill treatment did not denounce that moral vision. In fact, they said: "Given that moral vision, you have to respond to our quest for equality and justice if you are going to be faithful to yourself." I don't think there is any way you could just expunge that or strip that away. The question is how to guide it, and to shape it, and to think of it within a set of constraints so you don't turn a moral perspective into a huge moralistic crusade. There is a real distinction between the two of these. But to ask Americans to think of their foreign policy only in *realpolitik* terms is just an impossible thing to ask of them. You can't take away that strong notion of "we want to protect our own citizens, but we also want to help other people, we want to fight the bad guys, but we are not sure how much the cost should be because we are also worried about the cost for our own society – not just in materials and loss of life, but would it undermine our own understanding of ourselves?" All of that is in play when you are thinking about America and American politics, whether domestic or international.

Q: Focusing on the international side of American politics, would you agree that there is a general consensus across political affiliations that the American version of democracy should be disseminated all over the world? And that if there is any controversy, it arises mainly in regard to the question of how to disseminate it most effectively?

E: I think you are right about the bipartisan consensus that democracy promotion is in general a good idea. I do think, however, that there is more flexibility on exactly what makes a democracy. There is a big debate about that. Does the United States over-emphasize elections? What about a democratic civil society infrastructure, isn't that at least as important?

I am on the board of the National Endowment for Democracy, and this is an ongoing discussion on the board. Looking at particular societies and the advances that they have made in a more democratic direction, one of the things that is emphasized is governments that are accountable. Governments that have some responsibility to their people. That there is some transparency so citizens know what the government is doing. All of these are aspects of democracy promotion. I don't detect any real enthusiasm for the so-called 'cookie-cutter business' with a whole bunch of little Americas sitting everywhere – I don't detect much of that in the discussions that we have in D.C. It seems to me that there is a far more realistic understanding that democracies are going to be frail, and they are going to be imperfect where they haven't had them before. They are not going to look like the United States which is an old democracy by now, but nevertheless any movement toward protection of basic human rights and accountability and representation is a good thing. We should give people some slack if it doesn't look exactly like an ideal form we would like.

It is right that there is a general consensus along the lines you mentioned, but I think some of the Democrats who have been criticizing the Iraqi regime have been pretty harsh, too severe in condemning the leadership, saying they are not making the progress that we want them to make. I think one has to refrain a bit from being too severe when people are struggling in a difficult situation.

It is interesting that since the end of World War II the universal language in which people speak is the language of human rights. When people are grieved somewhere, they say their rights are being violated. That of course is historically a central element of democracy. There is a way in which certain democratic urgencies or tendencies are at this point universal – but that doesn't dictate the exact structure of what a regime is going to look like in any given society.

Q: How important is it that the United States maintains its position – and acceptance – as the sole superpower in the world? A quote from chapter 12, entitled 'American power and responsibility', seems to reflect the importance of this issue in your book: "Sometimes the most effective new frameworks are old ones resituated in a new reality. That is why some have called for a return of imperialism – not the bad old imperialism [...] rather the sort of imperialism [with] the world's great superpower taking on an enormous burden and doing so with a relatively, though not entirely, selfless intent."

E: The example you offer got me into a lot of trouble with some people because they took it as an unambiguous endorsement of imperialism. What I was really trying to say there is that if we look back on the whole scope of human history, some of the older imperial projects by comparison to certain alternatives don't look too bad. Some have made the argument that, all in all, with the Austro-Hungarian empire, the hand rested rather lightly when you look at the travail that followed its break-up. It wasn't like later totalitarianism. It wasn't the kind of society you and I would want to live in.

Today many hold the notion that there must be some responsible power involved in trying to stop the worst things that are going on. Is that imperialism? I don't know what to call it. You can imagine, for example, that in Sub-Saharan Africa today, it would be far better to have a power that has responsibility and some enforcement capacity to stop the almost routine slaughters that we see happening. That is an imagined alternative that is not going to happen because who wants to take on that job? It would be a thankless job.

A Polish friend of mine said: "It is almost impossible being the superpower because you are damned if you do, and you are damned if you don't." If you say: "We have got to get rid of Saddam Hussein," you are damned. But if you say: "We have done as much as we can about Darfur for the time being, we tried to encourage the UN, we have done this and that," you are damned because you haven't done enough. It is a very difficult position to be in. And I am not assuming that it is a permanent one. There are always going to be other powers that will rise in the world. We don't know the exact shape or form that will take, with the Chinese obviously becoming more powerful. But certainly, there is no denying the fact that the United States has been the primary enforcer of order in the world post World War II, and that is a role that most people – even though they won't say this publicly – are pretty glad that the US has played: Trying to maintain as much peace in the sense of not-open conflict as possible. The US has really been called upon to play that role – and it is a pretty thankless one in many respects. Western Europe obviously benefited from what the US did because Europe didn't have to pay for its own defense for half a century and could enjoy a real peace benefit that would otherwise have been unavailable.

It seems to me that 9/11 opened up a whole range of issues for consideration that were pretty anathema before. There were people like Michael Ignatieff talking about empire, and it is impossible to imagine him doing that ten years earlier. What measures can or should be taken with these substate actors who are so terribly dangerous and who have already done so much damage? When I am talking about why they loathe us in my book – "changes in our policies would not satisfy Islamists, the reason is quite basic: They loathe us because of who we are and what our society represents" –, it is not so much that we are a superpower. Looking at us from an Islamist radical position, we are terrible people, degraded, debauched – all you have to do is read Osama bin Laden's fatwa, and the whole thing is there. Just the mere presence of an American on the soil of the Saudi kingdom pollutes it. There are very primitive ideas of purity and pollution at work. I don't think it was "the US are too powerful and we are going to cut them down to size." It was "the US embodies everything that we find horrifying" – religious tolerance, too, for that matter, or pluralism. That is the point I wanted to make against those who said it is our specific policies they are objecting to. That is not where the argument lies, coming from the side of Islamism. It is really a religious project. People forget that and think Al-Qaeda are classical rational actors in a way they assume states are – and it is just not true. One of the things it is hard for modern secular intellectuals to come to grips with is that these people have a will to die – as bin Laden himself has articulated, "we will defeat you because your young people want to live, and ours want to die" – and we can't wrap our minds around that. It seems like that can't be true, he must really be objecting to American policy. But I think it is true, and this is the thing that is hardest to come to grips with.

Q: Zooming back in on the United States, how do you evaluate the importance of public deliberation as a feature of democracy? Where do you see today's intellectuals in this process?

E: Public deliberation is an essential feature. But unlike some people who have written about rational deliberation or deliberative democracy – they say certain conditions have to pertain, and people have to be informed about this and that – I cut people some slack. I think public deliberation takes place when people are sitting at Starbucks having coffee, when mothers are at the playground, watching their kids playing and talking about what is happening in the world. There are all these informal points of public deliberation so it doesn't have to be this kind of highly academic enterprise, everyone having lofty thoughts. I think it takes place all the time informally, especially in an election cycle, but also more generally. This is a form of public deliberation.

In a democracy, you need to guarantee that there is an open social civic world so that people just living their ordinary lives are going to have opportunities for these kinds of discussions. Intellectuals can help to shape and form that discussion, help people to get perspectives and categories to aid them in their process of thinking about some of these things, but I don't think it is our job to make it conform to a certain ideal. It is a messy informal process, and that is just fine.

Q: Professor Elshtain, thanks a lot for taking time out to speak with me.

E: You are very welcome. Good luck with what you are doing.

Francis Fukuyama

Bernard L. Schwartz Professor of International Political
Economy
Director, International Development Program
The Paul H. Nitze School of Advanced International Studies
Johns Hopkins University, Washington, D.C.

Q: Professor Fukuyama, what audience do you have in mind for your publications?

F: I've always tried to balance a couple of competing audiences. Obviously, as an academic you have to do things that are respectable academically, and that is a big problem because of the compartmentalization of all the disciplines. I don't know whether the trend is worse over time, or whether you just remember things differently, but it does seem to me that the whole tenure system and the way the academy works discourages people being innovative, it discourages them from writing in plain English other people can read because usually you want to please your people in the small sub-discipline – that's what is necessary to get tenure and that's why everybody feels they have to write like that. And it is very hard to cut across disciplines because each discipline has its own methodology, and they are very rigid about its application.

And so if you want to break out of that there is a second audience which I would say is not the general public. It is a kind of an informed general readership that likes to think about things, they tend to listen to National Public Radio, they think of themselves as concerned citizens, they are curious about things and so forth. That is a much broader audience. I think in the United States, in foreign affairs there is actually this deliberate effort that began after World War I to cultivate that audience. There is a big fight with the isolationists and there is a deliberate effort made by the elites in the country to create this network of councils of foreign affairs, and in every second or even third tier city, leading figures in the city would try to organize this kind of organization to force concerned citizens to actually pay attention to international politics because obviously that is pretty difficult.

The United States is such a self-sufficient country that we have gone along for a long time without worrying about anyone outside our particular little region. I think that has decayed a little bit during the Cold War, there was a lot of effort put into this, exchanges and so forth. But since the end of the Cold War, that has all kind of tapered off, but there still is that residual audience. And so those are basically the two that I try to straddle. And usually the strategy is: I try to bury the stuff for the academics in footnotes and keep the rest of it relatively free of jargon.

Q: In your work, do you try to provide the American public with a basic frame of political knowledge that will allow them to be informed, concerned citizens able to participate effectively in democracy? Do you have a kind of 'education project' in mind?

F: It is not on my mind particularly. It does seem to me that in any free society that is what ends up happening. I guess the problem these days is that there is so much information out there, it is very hard – if you don't really have a formal, higher education – to sort out what's worthwhile from what's useless, not credible.

Q: How would you define the term 'public intellectual'? Is it still an appropriate term these days? Is it still a term that points to something relevant?

F: It probably does. I would have to think about an exact definition. But I do think that in the United States, unlike Europe, or Japan, or other developed countries, it has always been a lot easier to move in and out of policy-making positions and the government. The particular way I came to this, when I graduated from Harvard, I did not seek an academic career. I went to the RAND Corporation, I worked there for ten years. RAND does public policy research. At the end of every RAND publication you got a section saying 'policy recommendation one, two, three, four'. They all have to be things that are actionable, that realistically a government agency could take and implement and so forth. So the government cultivated a number of these institutions, and then various political entrepreneurs of various ideologies realized that this was an important way to influence public policy. So you create this whole think-tank world out there. You have got this culture in Washington now with this alternation of administrations. When the Democrats are out of power, they all go to Brookings or Carnegie or some place like that. And when the Republicans are out of power, they go to AEI or Heritage. And so there is a large infrastructure that is set up. And plus, we politicize a much larger number of posts that in Europe would be civil service professional positions, and so in the Pentagon or State Department with every change of administration you have this huge turnover of fairly senior people. So I think that in a certain sense the existence of a public intellectual is dependent on a kind of institutional infrastructure that actually provides an outlet for people who normally would be much more academic or theoretical than actually have some say over real policy.

Q: If one looks back over history, the American intellectual seems to have lived with a certain tension from the beginning. On the one hand, there is a need for detachment, for a position somewhat distanced from society in order to come up with an outsider's view; to have a disinterested, not too prejudiced judgment. On the other hand, there is the desire to intervene, to act as a critical corrective, and have an impact on practical politics. What do you make of this tension given that so many intellectuals these days are employed by the government, or affiliated with a university or a think tank?

F: I remember having this argument with a number of Germans over this question whether it is ever legitimate for an intellectual to actually go into the government and serve in a policy-making position – doesn't this compromise your integrity and so forth? I have to say that doesn't really bother me all that much. I think that there is a definite danger that as an intellectual you become much more of a policy advocate and you use your intellectual powers to prove something that you know already rather than trying to search for what is true. But it is a big marketplace, and there are some people like that, but there are other people who aren't that hungry for immediate impact, and others that are more purely academic. And I think as long as all those categories exist – it is not preferable to have a world in which nobody feels that they should sully themselves by actually advising or using power.

Q: Turning to more recent history, we come across the term postmodernity – a term that carries a predominant notion of relativism. What do you make of this notion given the fact that everybody who publishes a book of the sort we're talking about claims a certain validity to what he or she says?

F: I think that postmodernism as a philosophical school is almost irrelevant to the way that public intellectuals work. I actually studied with Jacques Derrida and Roland Barthes and a number of these people when I was just out of graduate school. It always struck me that there is a real kind of hypocrisy in their positions because on the one hand they argued on an abstract level that there is no such thing as facts, there is only interpretations, but then they are committed Marxists or they still have a very definite political agenda, and they never bothered to reconcile that. And I think that for most Americans, they are much more pragmatic, and they don't start from a point of accepting some philosophical school, they begin with much less abstract kinds of principles.

Q: Taking another step toward the present, would you say that the authority of American intellectuals has increased since September 11? Might this be due to a public demand for a guiding voice of reason that will explain to them their nation's position in a changing world?

F: Yes, I think there is no question about that. In the 1990s, there wasn't really a set of hardly contested public issues. I mean we had these culture wars and technology, but not any kind of sharp divisions over foreign policy. Now there clearly is this big gap, the way it has been filled I am not sure it has been all that great. Obviously, we have got these huge gaps in our understanding of the Muslim world, and I think a lot of what has filled that space has not been all that helpful, but sure it has created a big demand for that kind of literature.

Q: Do you feel that there is a lack of explanation on the part of the government? Of what representatives of the government do?

F: I mean what country ever just accepts what the government says, especially when you got these big dramatic events, policies that don't look like they are terribly successful?

Q: Is there a need for someone to translate to the citizenry what the people in power do?

F: That's just kind of basic democratic theory. You don't live in a democracy if you accept anything that the government tells you. But that's not something new, it has been a permanent feature of free societies, it seems to me.

Q: Why do you choose a position somewhat beyond, somewhat outside practical politics?

F: Because I just didn't like being a bureaucrat. I found that it takes too much time, and I just found that given what I am good at, it wasn't the best use of my abilities.

Q: I'd like to read a quote from your book State-Building *to you: "The effort to be more scientific than the underlying subject matter permits carries a real cost in blinding us to the real world complexities, in this case of public administration as it is practiced in different societies." Could we carry this idea to a different level and say that there is a danger in being too specific or too scientific about something?*

F: What I am really referring to is the dominance of neo-classical economics in American social sciences. This is a really American phenomenon, I think it is much less common in Europe, or in Asia or in other parts of the world with big academic establishments, although it is infecting a lot of other places. For reasons that I don't completely understand there is such a desire to turn the study of politics and the other parts of the social sciences into something resembling the rigor of the natural sciences. I think these economists have pushed out other approaches to the study of human behavior. So all of the most prestigious universities are now captured by these people, Harvard, Stanford, Princeton, and so forth. I think there has been regression in the social sciences because the result of that is people build these far more mathematical models that are way oversimplified – they don't study languages, culture, history, the sorts of things social scientists used to pay attention to. As a result of this, we don't actually know how society in the Middle East works. We don't train students to spend time to learn that kind of thing. It is not a higher philosophical issue. It's just that Americans were always more in this British empiricist tradition than Europeans, and I think in some respects that is good because we actually take data seriously. We think that you actually have to produce some evidence to make an argument, which is not the case with a lot of European intellectuals. But on the other hand, there is a kind of fetishism about it that I think has actually made a lot of academic economics irrelevant.

Q: Now that you mention European intellectuals, is there a specific type of American intellectual?

F: No, I don't think there is a specific type. We also have our postmodernists and people in cultural studies. But I do think that this kind of hyper-empiricist type of social scientist really does not exist – I mean you have enclaves in economics departments in Europe, but as a general approach to the social sciences, I think it is much less common.

Q: I'd like to move on to the issue of morality in politics. Another book you wrote – America at the Crossroads. Democracy, Power, and the Neoconservative Legacy *– I find highly interesting because the title covers so much. I have the impression that America is also at a moral crossroads these days. Do you think it is the task of an authority somewhat beyond the fray of everyday politics to look out for these moral aspects?*

F: I think everybody is basically driven by these moral concerns on all sides. I think that is kind of a starting point.

Q: So there is no need for academia – a profession not involved in practical politics – to keep this in check?

F: That assumes that there is no moral case on the other side and that people are somehow just pursuing kind of base interests and you need these enlightened people to tell you that that is really wrong. I just don't think that is the way these things work. The Iraq War is a good case. There is a pretty strong moral case to be made for invading Iraq. And I think people that said: "Don't do it under any conditions" – it is just inherently wrong and not morally serious.

Q: Would you agree that there is general agreement across party boundaries and political affiliations that the American version of democracy should be disseminated all over the world – and that if there is controversy, it arises mainly in regard to how to proceed most effectively with this dissemination?

F: That's largely correct. The only issue is 'the American version' because I am not quite sure as opposed to a European version or Japanese version...

I am on the board of the National Endowment for Democracy which does democracy promotion. And that organization has very, very strong bipartisan support. We support building parliamentary proportional representation and European style systems in certain parts of the world, so I am not quite sure what you mean by 'American style of democracy' as opposed to other types of democracy.

Q: To clarify, let me read you another quote from your book State-Building: *"When President Reagan repeatedly quoted Winthrop in speaking of the United States as a 'shining city on a hill', his words had great resonance for many Americans. This feeling leads at times to a typically American tendency to confuse its own national interests with the broader interests of the world as a whole." Could you go into this a little more?*

F: It has to do with American exceptionalism. The United States does feel that it is not just an ordinary country, but that it is somehow the harbinger of a greater universal movement toward democracy. I think that has been true ever since the founding of the American Republic. There is this tendency to see our own actions in the most favorable possible light, and therefore not to be able to perceive the way that other people don't agree with that interpretation; they see us acting out of much more self-interested motives. You hear this on the Right in this country all the time, people say "why can't these Muslims understand – we have helped them so much, we have done nothing but good for them, and they are so ungrateful to us for having done that." And obviously, if you go to the Middle East, that is not remotely the perception of how the United States has behaved.

Q: Given this self-perception of parts of the American public, and the sheer fact that their nation is the only remaining superpower, two questions come to mind: First, how important is it that the US remain the sole superpower? Second, how should the US go about explaining their reasoning on this issue?

F: I don't think that there is any way that the United States concept for itself the goal of remaining the sole superpower. This famous defense guidance that Paul Wolfowitz presided over at the end of the first Bush administration where they talked about the United States remaining predominant – that view just never struck me as remotely realistic because how are you going to prevent the rise of China as a superpower? There is no way of doing that. So as an explicit object of policy I don't think that that's in the cards. I do think that American power is important, but how it is used is quite up for grabs.

My own personal view is that if you are going to be as powerful as we are and you want to influence people you have got to be a little bit more subtle about the way you exercise power. In *America at the Crossroads* I cited Bismarck as an example of someone that understood that a unified

Germany would be very threatening to the rest of Europe and therefore tried to minimize the degree to which that power is exercised. I think China has been doing that as well. They have realized that their rise is threatening to all their Asian neighbors. So they have taken a lot of steps to try to disguise that. I think we have kind of done the opposite. We have said "we are the biggest on the block, we are going to do what we want." I just think that that's been a terrible mistake. Because I don't think you can avoid the exercise of American power and in some cases it will be very worthwhile, but if you rub people's noses in the fact of how strong the United States is, it makes them less willing to work with you.

Q: Could you elaborate a little more on the question of how the United States should convey what they do to the countries they affect? Is there a lack of explanation?

F: I think the Bush administration corrected a lot of that in the second term. If you look at the way we have approached North Korea or Iran: Once Condolezza Rice moved over to the State Department, it has been very multilateral and cooperative, and indeed on Iran there has been a lot of US-European cooperation, similarly in Asia, the six-party-talks...

I think that there is no fundamental clash of values or interests in most of these issue areas between the US and Europe. And given that Europe meets the United States and vice versa in a lot of these cases, there ought to be a lot of relatively pragmatic cooperation. So I think the failure of that in the Iraq War – it was partly that that case itself was a hard one to make, but I also think that the way that it was made was unnecessarily offensive and it was a kind of self-defeating project therefore.

Q: For my last question, I would like to zoom back in on the United States and ask you about a feature of today's democracy: How do you evaluate the importance of public deliberation? Where do you locate the intellectuals in this?

F: If you have a country of 300 million people, it is hard to have a deliberative democracy of the sort they had in Athens and New England town meetings. It is a big kind of an institutional problem: How do you actually generate real public discussion as opposed to simply people registering their preferences and politicians aggregating those preferences? And I think that is probably where public intellectuals play a fairly big role because there is a discussion that takes place in the media, different points of view are argued out. I would say not enough viewpoints are repre-sented, and the argument is not serious enough often times, but I don't know what else you would do, and I do think it is extremely important that that kind of argument happened. There has been actually a very good outpouring of books about foreign policy over the last five years – if you go to the bookstore, there is just a pile of them, talking about what went wrong, how do you do it better next time. That's all I think part of the public discussion that really needs to happen.

Q: Professor Fukuyama, thanks a lot for taking the time to speak with me.

F: Thank you, and good luck with your studies.

Robert O. Keohane

Professor of International Affairs
Woodrow Wilson School
Princeton University, NJ

Q: Professor Keohane, what audience do you have in mind for your publications? Do you reach out beyond the academy to the broader, educated public?

K: It depends on the publication. With the Castle Lectures I gave at Yale University in the fall of 2007, I was thinking of people who were not political scientists. I wrote those and gave those with the sort of person you were mentioning in mind: Members of the broad, educated public. But my own work has mostly been directed at political scientists. So this is a kind of different departure for me. I've been trying to think about what the implications are of the world view I have for how institutions ought to be designed, which of course has some implications for the questions of US policy. *After Hegemony* was written strictly for political scientists. I didn't expect it to be read as much as it has been. But it was read almost entirely inside the discipline. It's difficult. People who are not studying political science or international relations don't get very far with it. And that's certainly true of my book with King and Verba, *Designing Social Inquiry*, and it's true of *Power and Interdependence*. For the Castle Lectures and the book I'm presumably going to produce from them, I have a broader audience in mind.

Q: With this broader public in mind, do you have the intention of educating your audience? Do you try to provide American citizens with a frame of knowledge concerning international relations so they will be in a better position to judge American foreign policy and other aspects of political life?

K: Yes. I think the best public intellectuals – I am not one of them – do that a lot and very well. Like my Dean Anne-Marie Slaughter, my colleague John Ikenberry. People who write very frequently for *Foreign Affairs*, for example, do exactly that kind of publication apart from their writings in academic journals. These articles do not have any references, the work is usually not very original, from a theoretical point of view, but is written for a magazine read by people who are intelligent observers. I only published once there, about ten years ago, and I was struck by how many people including the former president of Princeton paid attention to that piece. Not a huge number, but the breadth was very different.

Q: How would you define the term public intellectual?

K: There is a very good piece by Richard Lewontin in the current *New York Review of Books*, where he talks about Stephen Jay Gould as a public intellectual. Lewontin says that the best public intellectuals are those people who tend to come up with the knowledge they have on the basis of some actual accomplishments and to explain it in a way that is accessible to a broad public, but that is also consistent with the science. Gould certainly had that feature, Carl Sagan had that characteristic. I think the danger of being a public intellectual is to sort of sound off on your own opinions, when there is not a lot of basis for them. I think being a public intellectual is a valuable role played by social scientists and international lawyers like Slaughter but it is a tricky role because in our field the quality or certainty of that scientific knowledge is much lower, and the temptation to inject one's political views under the cover of academic authority is much greater. So I am not surprised that people often don't take the public intellectuals that come out of political science as seriously as they take Carl Sagan or Steve Gould.

Q: But you would still deem the term itself appropriate these days?

K: I think it is an appropriate term. You wouldn't want to assume that a public intellectual is saying something not worth listening to, any more than you would assume that you should believe his or her claims. And it is not a term that is to do with being either on the Right or the Left. Robert Kagan and William Kristol are public intellectuals on the Right, just as Slaughter and Ikenberry are public intellectuals on the moderate Left. There are two questions to ask, first: What is the quality of the analysis they are doing? That's independent of their academic authority. Much of this analysis looks like what high-class journalists would do. If you took the name off, you might not be able to tell. So for example I think the best

book on globalization is Martin Wolf's book *Why Globalization Works*.
Martin Wolf is a journalist. Jagdish Bhagwati is a public intellectual, and
he is a fire-fine economist, but in my view, his book on globalization – *In
Defense of Globalization* – is not nearly as good as Wolf's. So it doesn't
necessarily mean that even the very talented public intellectuals are always going to be better than the journalists.

The other dimension is whether there really is technical knowledge
that is brought across, in a way that it illuminates the issue. Larry Sum-
mers now comments in the *Financial Times*, and I always find that he
really brings a depth of economic knowledge and analysis to that commentary that sets it apart and above most other commentaries I have seen
on economic analysis. So some intellectuals will have that gift of boiling
down something which really is insightful, although you have to differen-
tiate between what they say that is based on science, and what they say
that is based on just their opinion.

*Q: Intellectuals seem to be caught up in a difficult predicament. On the one
hand, they claim to have a distanced point of view that allows for less-
biased judgment on matters of society and politics. On the other hand, they
claim to intervene and possibly act as a critical corrective. What do you
make of this paradox, given the fact that, today, so many intellectuals are
employed by universities, the government, or think tanks?*

K: I think there is a real tension. I wouldn't have said it is a paradox. A
paradox is a contradiction by its own terms. It is a real tension, and I have
been aware of it for a long time. I don't think that being part of the university is problematic for it. And most people who are in government
wouldn't be considered public intellectuals as long as they are in the government. They have to speak for the government then. Everyone knows
their speeches are cleared. But outside of government I don't think there
is anything problematic about any intellectual who is in the university
speaking out on any public issue. That's what they certainly have a right
to do, if they want to do it. They have no obligation to. In many universities, it is not what you get paid for, what you are awarded for. So you
don't find very many untenured political scientists writing public intellectual stuff because you don't get tenure for it. So it is something that
comes when you already have tenure.

I have deliberately decided for most of my career not to write opinion
pieces. The reason is not that I am not involved politically – I was very

active against the Vietnam War, but there is nothing in my body of writing on this. Until the Iraq War, I did almost nothing that would be considered public intellectual apart from a couple of articles on foreign policy, in *Foreign Affairs* and others. But they were very close to the kind of research I was doing, and so only different in style since I was speaking to a general audience – not advocacy. I think when you get into advocacy, you must make a choice. If you are in advocacy, like a politician, you develop commitments. And you have a public record for something, which makes it very difficult to change your mind unless you are willing to be accused of being inconsistent by your adversaries. Which is why in politics, people have a very hard time reacting to new facts because they have committed themselves to a certain view.

In general, public intellectuals writing on world politics tend to be people who would like to be in power. Joseph Nye, Anne-Marie Slaughter, John Ikenberry – these are people who either have or would like to wield political power. And one reason they speak up on *Foreign Affairs* is not just to have a voice and make a contribution, but to make a record so they can be seen as people who have leading voices on a subject. The problem is that this ambition may lead people to start calculating what to say and what not to say and to be tempted to go with their audience. It is not surprising in this connection that the public intellectuals speaking on international relations were more favorable toward the Iraq War than most political scientists. The prevailing belief was that opposing the Iraq War would be a political death sentence. With all the politicians going that way, some public intellectuals at least hedged their bets.

Q: Turning to the recent past, we come across a period in history that has been named 'postmodernity'. Its predominant feature is a notion of relativism, i.e. the ultimate, universal truth and certainty of anything is very much disputed or simply claimed to be non-existent. Do you feel this to be true? And if so, does it have any influence on your work?

K: In my view the notion of postmodernity is pretty much nonsense. I think there was a wave, very strong from the early eighties to the mid-nineties, of relativism in the social sciences. It was extremely strong in anthropology. It made some impact in political science, none at all in economics. It didn't make much effect in moral philosophy. To say that the validity of empirical statements, positive statements, is always uncertain is a platitude. These people discovered the platitude, and thought they had made a discovery because they thought that somehow scientists thought that things were certain. But they didn't know anything about science. The first principle of science is that nothing is certain. So the critics' premise was false, they simply didn't know what they were talking about. Alternatively, the proposition was that normative statements cannot be grounded in a way that makes them certain, or even susceptible to being proven true or false. But we have known that for very many centuries. It has certainly been known and believed since Hume and Spinoza.

I think the peak in postmodern thinking in US political science came ten years ago. Such a way of thinking doesn't have much value politically or socially, and it is – from a natural science point of view – manifestly in conflict with the fact that we have much more control of the world, for better or worse, that comes out of science. The critical point was the 1996 Sokal's Hoax, a satirical pseudo-attack on science from a postmodernist point of view – a hoax by physicist Alan Sokal perpetrated on the editorial staff and readership of Duke University's postmodern cultural studies journal *Social Text*. It was acclaimed by many postmodernists as being very important. It was entirely a spoof, and they didn't realize it. And he then decoded it for them. I think Sokal revealed the emptiness of this stuff.

Q: Let's take one step further toward the present: What is the situation like for intellectuals since 9/11? Has their authority increased again, possibly because of a demand for orientation on the part of an American public in need of guidance?

K: Not in the immediate aftermath of 9/11 – quite the contrary. One of the least reported facts of the Iraq War run-up was that there was a petition signed by over a thousand professional students of international relations ranging from John Mearsheimer to me, and everybody on the left of me, opposing the Iraq War. The media did not regard it as news that almost all professional students of international relations in the United States thought that attacking Iraq was a bad idea. So I don't think that we have much influence. I get more attention for my work in Europe and China than in the United States.

Q: How do you perceive the relation between the academic world and the world of 'hands-on politics' – what's the balance of power like between the two?

K: The balance of power is all on the side of the hands-on politics people. The United States is a very big country. There are lots of people who are clamoring for the ear of policy makers and for the ear of publics. And furthermore, academia in this country is more technically oriented, more scientifically oriented, and less policy-oriented than academia in most other countries. In political science, there is a huge divergence between what the journals talk about and what the public talks about. There was a special issue of *International Organization* in 1998, looking back over the last 50 years of the journal, where it became clear that in the 1960s – this might not have been very good political science – there was a lot of commentary on policy which could have been read and absorbed by a policy-maker in the evening, which was not true by 1998. There was very little comment on policy, and much of it could only be understood with a background in the field. So there has been an increasing bifurcation. In the 1950s, some of the leading lights of academic international relations, George Kennan, Hans Morgenthau, and Bernard Brodie, for example, were interested in policy and had some influence on policy, but they were also major figures in the academy. I can't think of many people now who are both political scientists of note and people with foreign policy influence. Joseph Nye comes to mind, and maybe John Ikenberry.

Q: Is there perhaps a different kind of power available to academia? A power that might take shape in being in a position to conceptualize the terms that are then used in the public policy debate?

K: Yes, I believe that in the long term we have an impact, although in the short term we don't have it. What John Maynard Keynes said – "madmen in authority" –, I think he was right about that: "Madmen in authority, who hear voices in the air, are distilling their frenzy from some academic scribbler of a few years back." He was thinking of Marx, I think, but it was certainly true of himself. There is a sense that if the analysis of world politics captures something that in a sense is true about it or captures a leading edge of change that is then seen as more and more important, I think that the analysis gets incorporated into ordinary language and that people who have never read the theorist and don't even know who the theorist is are actually speaking in his voice. That's certainly true of Schelling's strategy of conflict by 1960. That's true of Nye's soft power idea, and I think it is true of Nye's and my notion of asymmetrical interdependence and power. Or maybe the concept of interdependence, but not the phrase.

It is always hard to see: Are scholars working their way into the public consciousness, or are they just paralleling other people figuring this out, and so it would be independent streams. But either way, there is this impact. And I do believe that policy makers have to have some sort of theory that they work with. It orders the world for them. And my most important career mission in life is to get people think not in terms of the old realist theory but in a different, more institutionalist way so they see possibilities they would not otherwise see. As an example, the Chinese are thinking that way now but they weren't at all ten years ago.

Q: "I define the phrase 'the globalization of informal violence'. In referring to a general category of action, I substitute this phrase for 'terrorism', since the latter concept has such negative connotations that it is very difficult to define in an analytically neutral and consistent way that commands general acceptance" – this is a quote from the last chapter of Power and Governance in a Partially Globalized World. *Do you see it as your task to conceptualize certain terms through which the world can then be perceived?*

K: In political science we deal with issues that William Connolly once called 'essentially contested concepts'. 'Power' is a classic example. There is no stable definition of power. It means many different things probably because it is so intrinsic to the way we think about the world and the way we behave. 'Class' is another example. And terrorism is like that in a way. It is so loaded and it is so important for political leaders rhetorically that there is not going to be agreement on this. It is not like the atomic weight of silver which is a known quantity. That is what I was trying to say. If we are going to think about this issue clearly, we may not be able to enforce a common agreement on what terrorism is and therefore we may need to use a different language to be clear.

But the more you want to be heard, the more you have to use conventional language. That language is necessarily imprecise, and you don't control it because the reader comes to it with a whole series of preconceptions. So when you say 'globalization' or 'terrorism', even if you define it, they are not going to pay attention, they already *know* what 'globalization' and 'terrorism' is. So there is a trade-off there. You are trading off precision, you are probably trading off originality since you get trapped into a conventional way of looking at a problem. But what you are getting is some ability to connect up with the reader who is going to pay attention. So there is a real trade-off there.

Q: Why did you choose a position in the academic world, which is more removed from practical politics?

K: It is in my academic autobiography, in my book *International Institutions and State Power*. I was raised in an academic family. And I considered doing something else, but I always found that my temperament is best suited to being an academic. Once I went to graduate school, I didn't look back. Because my real love in graduate school was political theory. I am not really a policy wonk, I am a theorist, by temperament and interest. I don't read *Foreign Affairs* very much. And I don't think I am very good at that kind of bureaucratic strategies – seeing what someone is going to throw at you next, what maneuver they are going to do. If I had been in policy, I would have been chewed up. I wouldn't have seen what's coming, some plot was laid, I wouldn't even have known it was coming. Joseph Nye is much better at that. He is a very honest person, but he is much better at seeing 'politically'.

Q: Would you say that an authority somewhat outside of politics should keep an eye on the moral issues involved in politics?

K: I think we all need to be concerned with moral issues. And a fair amount of my work obviously shows this, you can see quite a bit of discussion of this here and there. But I would distinguish quite sharply between having moral purposes and preaching. Social science is problematic enough as science. It is hard to justify unless you have a moral purpose for doing it. If I didn't have a moral purpose in doing social science, I would be a physicist or a biologist. I would actually learn something with more ability to interpret that you are right, something where more scientific progress takes place. If you are interested in pure knowledge, you shouldn't be in this business. What would be the point unless you are just terrible at everything else? There has to be some overall moral purpose.

My overall moral purpose is to try to improve the amount of international cooperation that takes place in the world and make leading people think differently about how they could do it. And one hopes that it makes them see more opportunities and also make fewer mistakes in their actions. That's the overall purpose of my work and it has been there for thirty years. But I am very much against moralizing – as a scholar. As an individual, in private conversation, I moralize all the time, ranting about someone who behaves badly and so on. But I try to avoid writing as a scholar in a way that is really just moralizing. That seems to me not to be a scholarly activity. It is a perfectly reasonable private activity, and it is also a reasonable thing to do in the public realm. When the Iraq War came along, I wrote a bunch of op-ed pieces – that has never happened before. Because I am not a noted public intellectual, I wrote for the Raleigh, North Carolina, *News and Observer*, not for the *New York Times*. But entering the public arena on Iraq was for me an exception because of the importance of the issue and the obvious error of our ways.

Q: I would like to move on a little bit and discuss some of the content of the Castle Lectures you gave at Yale. You made a remarkably clear distinction between the issues of efficacy and design on the one hand, and the normative issues on the other.

K: That's certainly American social science. I think that one has an obligation to separate what you believe are your empirical or positive propositions from your normative ones. As I said before, I also feel an obligation to have a normative purpose for your work as a whole. But if the normative ones creep into your empirical material, then you are in danger of doing bad empirical work which simply tries to find what you want to find. And that seems to me to be the antithesis of good social science.

Q: According to your talk at Yale, when it comes to designing international institutions, a number of precepts apply. Some of these you describe as 'normatively unproblematic', others seem to be 'normatively problematic'. Among the problematic ones is the following: "Powerful states that are committed to multilateral institutions should exert leadership, which means using their resources to induce others to participate constructively." Would you agree that there is a general consensus among American public intellectuals – with a small number of deviants – that the United States should remain in the leading position regarding multilateral institutions? And, in addition, would you agree that if there is any controversy surrounding the issue, it is concerned with how to exert this leadership most effectively?

K: I would agree with part of that. I think there is a general agreement among Americans, and it is not surprising, that it is a good thing for the US to be in a leading position. And obviously, there is a degree of self-interest in that. But there is also the long-standing American view that the United States plays a distinctive role in the world and that it has a distinctive political culture, philosophy, and history that allow it to lead the way throughout the world. But I think what is really an issue, and there is a big controversy, is what leadership means. Answering this question implies asking what the purpose of leadership is.

On the Right, there is a general view that the US should be true to itself. The advice is that of Polonius: "To thine own self be true." Represent American values, which are superior values, to the rest of the world. And try to propagate them, when possible without force, or with force, if you don't have a chance to do so. The world will be a better place if it is more like America. That's what leadership is: Standing tall.

My own view on leadership is that leadership does not presume that our society is by any means better than other societies. I think it is better than most non-democratic societies. I think that in some ways it is better than other democratic societies, in some ways worse, and in some ways just different. So to believe in US leadership doesn't require any assumption about moral superiority. What it does require is the assumption that the United States is capable of leading positively because it is a democracy with a liberal and free spirit of criticism. And that since the US is so big and so powerful, it has to lead if there is going to be effective action against a whole series of problems from global warming to terrorism. If the greatest democracy were not to try to exert leadership, there would be a very bad situation.

Q: Let me read you another one of the 'problematic precepts': "Institutional designers should make differential concessions to states, deferring more to those states whose participation is essential to make agreements effective." Does this refer to your statement that the US should be in a leading position and that institutional designers, in turn, should acknowledge that fact?

K: The statement does not just refer to the United States. In designing institutions, for example on climate change, you have to acknowledge that China is a big player. We may not like the Chinese view on climate, trade, or human rights, but we have to deal with it. By the same token,

American human rights policy is not the same toward Guatemala as toward China. That is unfair in some egalitarian sense, but it is reality. You might well implement a human rights policy that the Guatemalans really dislike, you have a much harder time when sampling what the Chinese are going to say. You pay a much bigger price. So that's just reality, not just for the US, but in fact, it is a general phenomenon.

Q: A concluding question on the domestic front concerns public deliberation in democracy. How would you evaluate its importance for the present-day concept of American democracy?

K: I am just working on a paper with Stephen Macedo and Andrew Moravcsik – "Democracy-Enhancing Multilateralism" – which talks about that a little bit. My conception of democracy is not a plebiscitary conception. Elections are an important component, but only one component for me. It is a very liberal, constitutional conception of democracy. And one of the essential elements of that is a multiple set of forms for deliberation to take place among different sets of actors – not closed to people who are experts, but sometimes restricted to only the people who have enough knowledge to participate in it. Maybe they are people who go to lectures at Yale. I think that is the essential part of it. I would not be in favor of a system, using the electronic voting, where we all vote on fifty issues a month. It is only going to be ignorance. Broadly speaking, I am sympathetic with the deliberative democrats – on most issues, deliberation in a pluralistic society, not a plebiscite, will yield the best policy. But the public must have the final say, through elections. However, we know that elections are typically fought on at most three or four issues, not fifty or a hundred or a thousand issues. And most of the decisions made by a democratic society on most issues should be made in some deliberative way. And that deliberation should be as much as possible public and transparent. It can't always be, if you are deliberating whether to spy on somebody, you can't do that. But those who are making the decisions should be accountable to people who can at least listen to what the deliberators said about it.

Q: Public intellectuals function as translators in this process?

K: At their best, they do. When I came to this school – Princeton's Woodrow Wilson School –, I came partly because I wanted to be in a place where there were people who were in a sense translators. I thought that maybe my voice would be a little bit amplified if people who were more effective at doing the public outreach were talking to me and I was talking to them.

Q: Professor Keohane, thank you very much for your time.

K: Thank you. I hope the interview was useful to you.

James M. Lindsay

Senior Vice President, Director of Studies, and Maurice R.
Greenberg Chair, Council on Foreign Relations (CFR)
New York City and Washington, D.C.

Q: Professor Lindsay, what audience do you have in mind for your publications?

L: With *America Unbound*, our goal was to reach people who are interested in the state of the debate in American foreign policy, and the future of America's role in the world. When you start a book like *America Unbound*, you know that most Americans are never going to read it. So by definition you are trying to capture the attention of the attentive public that follows political events. Within that attentive public, there are two segments: One are the ideologues – people who buy books by the Ann Coulters and Al Frankens of the world, people who are looking to have their prejudices confirmed by incendiary writing. And then there are people who want to be informed. Our book was aimed at people who wanted to be informed, as opposed being entertained or outraged.

Q: As for the ones who want to be informed, is there an intention to educate in what you do?

L: Certainly. Both Prof. Daalder and I are Ph.D.s by training, so the educational contributions of our writings are important to us. We were at Brookings when we wrote *America Unbound*, and part of the Brookings mission is to enrich, broaden, and enliven the public debate by explaining to people how the world is and how it operates. At Brookings, or the Council on Foreign Relations, a major part of the job of a Senior Fellow is educational, not just in the writings, but also in doing interviews with the news media. One thing that strikes me doing interviews with journalists is that they often know little about the subject in question. They have a deadline, and they have to write a story. Part of the job at a think tank is to help journalists understand what the issues are and how to frame them.

Q: How would you define the term 'public intellectual'? Does it still point to something relevant these days?

L: To me, the term 'public intellectual' signals somebody who sells more books than I do. I am not sure what it means to be a public intellectual. It is not a term I commonly use.

Q: Looking back at history, the American intellectual seems to have lived with a tension from the beginning: On the one hand, a need for critical distance, while on the other hand, a desire to intervene in society and make an impact. Is the intellectuals' claim to act somewhat outside of purpose-driven constraints problematic today, given their affiliation with academia, the government, and the think tanks?

L: I would describe it differently. If you go back fifty or sixty years, it was not uncommon for people to move back and forth, particularly between elite universities and the government. As the academy became more and more specialized, a dominant tribe emerged in academia that wanted to stand apart and had no interest in being involved in politics and government. The political science department at Yale was the point of the spear on this. And then there are other people coming out of academia who historically always wanted to be academics *and* to be involved in government policy. In some sense, Harvard represents the epitome of that. So the tension is not within the individual – 'Should I stay, or should I go', to quote *The Clash* – but rather between different communities in the academic world.

Many of my colleagues when I was at the University of Iowa were horrified when I went to the White House. In their view, that was a bad thing for a scholar to do. I don't think scholarship is harmed by actually having hands on experience with policymaking. In many ways it is better for government and for scholarship if people actually know what they are writing about. Otherwise you run the risk of being someone who extols the joys of driving a BMW or a Mercedes without ever having gotten behind the wheel of a car. So I don't see practical experience as a danger. It is a separate issue whether the advice that academics give is good or bad for the country.

Q: Given your professional experience in both government and academia, what does your audience expect from you? Concrete policy proposals, or rather a visionary framework of American ideals?

L: This gets us back to the point I mentioned about the tension between different communities of scholars. When you come back to an academic environment, people want you to publish in academic journals, and they scratch their heads if you write for a broader audience. In my case, when I returned to academia I kept writing for the audiences I wrote for when I was at Brookings and the Council on Foreign Relations. There is a space out there – it is not being filled terribly well – which tries to take the best of what emerges from academic scholarship, our understanding of how the world works, and then blend that with an understanding of what it is government can do, and what it needs so it can do it. If you think of it in terms of communities, a public intellectual is somebody who tries to fill that niche. Academics are very good at explaining things, particularly to other academics, but they tend to fall short when it comes to translating an idea into action. So you run the risk that academic work just becomes self-absorbed – you are preaching to the choir. What public intellectuals can do is take good ideas and present them in terms that make them compelling, politically salable, politically manageable. Places like Brookings and the Council on Foreign Relations draw on people with good academic credentials who are in a sense bilingual: They can speak to scholars, but they also can speak to the broader public and policy makers.

Q: What is the balance of power like between the world of 'thinkers' and the world of 'doers'? A quote from your introduction seems to suggest that concepts developed in the realm of ideas do get picked up and acquire decisive power in practical politics: "George W. Bush delivered the revolution that Krauthammer urged. It was not a revolution that started, as many later have suggested, on September 11, 2001. The worldview that drove it existed long before..."

L: Yes, most certainly. That is how it works. When government officials, whether they are elected or appointed, come to office, they bring with them a stock of intellectual capital: Ideas, notions, or prejudices, depending upon their level of development. The ideas come from many places: courses in high school or college, reading a newspaper or novel, conversation at a cocktail party, something overhead on talk radio, or even experiences on the playground.

The Robert Kagans and Francis Fukuyamas of the world are in the business of both generating and propagating ideas. In some sense, they are sowing apple seeds: They are throwing out ideas, hoping they fall on some fertile soil and something takes root and prospers.

Policymakers often don't know a lot about many issues. If you serve on the National Security Council staff in the White House watching the National Security Adviser work, your first reaction is going to be: I can't believe how many issues there are. How can one person stay on top of so many issues? And the reality is you can't. This is why serving in government is so hard. You need to know what the specifics of the dispute between Columbia and Venezuela, what the particulars are of the rules governing the law of sea treaty, how China sees North Korea, and so forth. You also have to understand who in the bureaucracy wants to do what, as well as what the political consequences are of different decisions. It gets extraordinarily complicated. People work fourteen, sixteen, eighteen hour-days day in, day out, and they don't have a lot of time to reflect on what is happening or to participate in seminars talking about major trends in the world. They operate on the basis of the intellectual capital they bring with them.

That is why public intellectuals are important. They generate ideas. Just as important, they proselytize on behalf of their ideas, whether it is an argument for creating a league of democracy, or bringing back realism, or tackling the problem of climate change. They want to grab people. And often they grab people not with a long, exhaustive analysis of a problem, but with a catchy way of framing it: Robert Kagan's famous quip that 'Americans are from Mars, Europeans are from Venus' is a good example. Often it is a catchy framing mechanism, or a really good anecdote, that sells the idea you are pushing. Certainly these are ideas you believe in, and you are trying to persuade people to accept them.

If as a public intellectual you can persuade people who have influence, then you can affect policy. Think tanks like Brookings or the Council on Foreign Relations put a premium on writing op-eds for that reason. If you write a great book of 200 pages at Brookings, whether it is on health care, or America's role in the world, or why we should attack Iran, most people in the policy making world aren't going to read it. But if you write an op-ed in the *New York Times*, or the *Washington Post*, it may get a lot of play. Think of Ken Pollack and Michael O'Hanlon who wrote a piece a while back where they said that the surge in Iraq is working – something like that can get a lot of play because it is short, it is well-placed, and helpful to people who don't have a lot of time to go out and do their own diligent research to assess the situation.

Q: Has the authority of intellectuals increased since September 11, possibly due to a need for orientation on the side of the American public?

L: No. Public intellectuals and academics are like TV executives – they are victims or beneficiaries of trends rather than trendsetters. If you were writing on foreign policy in the 1990s, people mostly ignored you. Foreign policy just wasn't on people's radar screens. This is largely because rather than having Plato's philosopher king running the show we have a democracy. And if you look at the public opinion polls, foreign policy was at the bottom of the barrel in terms of the public's interest. In democracies politicians gravitate toward issues that the public cares about, and away from issues that the public doesn't have much interest in. If you look at the media coverage of foreign policy events in the 1990s, it was declining.

Obviously, September 11 made a big difference for everyone writing on foreign policy. It changed the frame for everybody. In some sense, the pendulum swung too far in the other direction – which explains a lot that happened in American foreign policy. If you were peddling a book proposal about the Jihadist threat to a publisher in August 2001, you would have had a lot of doors slammed in your face. After September 11 publishers were signing up those kinds of books left and right.

What you also want to talk about is how to be *effective* in terms of spreading ideas. People who write against type can be very, very effective. Ideas or arguments attract attention based not just on the message but on who the messenger is. During the run-up to the Iraq War, for example, Ken Pollack's *The Gathering Storm* got a lot of play – in part because of his argument, but also because he had worked in the Clinton administration and was now at Brookings, which is presumed to be a left-of-center 'say-no-to-war, we-want-diplomacy' kind of place. But Ken argued that Iraq was a very real threat and action needed to be taken. His message got an extra hearing because many people expected that someone with his background would have argued the opposite.

So the messenger can be as important as the message. And it may also be that something very smart coming out of Brookings or the Council on Foreign Relations gets dismissed on the grounds that it is "Brookings or the Council – they are all just out there in the middle of the road with all the yellow stripes and the dead armadillos." In the end, the appeal of the message you are trying to get out is partly tied to the intellectual power of your argument, but it is also going to be influenced by who you are, as well as people's perceptions of your home institution.

Q: A quote from the chapter 'The Bush Strategy': "The essence of the Bush strategy therefore was to use America's unprecedented power to remake the world in America's image." Is there a general consensus even across political affiliations that the American version of democracy should be disseminated in the world?

L: I disagree with the question as you phrase it, particularly with the phrase 'the American version of democracy' because I don't think it is the case that Americans have detailed thoughts on the appropriate way to set up a democratic political system – that is it should be a presidential system, bicameral, separation of powers, and so on. I don't think Americans have any particular desire to see the U.S. presidential system imposed on other places.

If you rephrase your question as a belief that the world would be better off if all people got to choose their leaders, and that they not only got the right to vote in elections but also the right to live under the rule of law based on liberal constitutional principles, then, yes, I think most Americans would say that is a good idea. I am not sure they would know why that would be a good idea, but they would intuitively think it is a good idea.

In the chapter on the Iraq policy, 'The Aftermath', Prof. Daalder and I try to make a distinction between the process – the procedures by which the government operated – and the substance – what that government did. The Bush administration had the vision that they were going to go in, essentially get the bad guys, and a well-functioning, pro-western government would take their place. It was a case of magical thinking: If we hope hard enough, it will happen! There was no logic behind it.

If you were to go to most Americans – which is part of what the Bush administration did – and say "we are going to get rid of the bad guys, and if we get rid of them, the result will be good," they would think that is terrific. All political messages take place in a culture in which there are all kinds of unspoken historical references. In many ways, the Bush administration discussed Iraq like it was a Hollywood western. Think of *High Noon* or dozens of other films where the town is held hostage by evil men, and the hero – John Wayne, Gary Cooper – rides into town and kills the bad guy. Once the bad guy is taken out, the town is happy again, the hero rides off into the sunset, and the town is basking in its new found freedom. Americans tend to think that the kind of well-functioning, well-institutionalized democratic government they have is natural, the default position. Whereas for countries with different historical experiences and cultural referents, that seems wildly optimistic if not kooky.

Q: How important is it that the United States remains the only super-power?

L: Ultimately, the United States cannot maintain a position of being the only superpower in the world. It is not the only one who has a say in that. What the Chinese choose to do, what happens in India, what happens in the international global system, what happens with climate change – there are lots of things that happen that will influence the course of American dominance, or how long it lasts, and how effective it can be.

My preference as an American would be that American primacy last as long as possible. Obviously, any country wants to control as much of its external environment as possible – that is a natural sort of thing.

But the issue of American dominance is not the key one. The big issue at the end of the day is: What is the wisest way for America to navigate its way in the world? It is possible both for America to remain the dominant power and to have a less interventionist, less counterproductive foreign policy. To some extent Robert Kagan is right: By virtue of the fact that the United States is the biggest, most powerful country, there is going to be a certain set of expectations that it act in a particular way, and when it doesn't, everybody gets unhappy. I am not sure whether everyone would be really excited if the United States suddenly said "ok, we are going to revert to 1930s-style isolationism – you all take care."

I have seen this ambivalence in my conversations over the years with foreign visitors. When I was at Brookings, we would meet with visiting delegations from Latin America. Their complaint was: "You Americans intervene too much in our region, you are always meddling our politics, would you just leave us alone?" A few years later at the Council on Foreign Relations I remember having a delegation from Latin America. This was at a time when the Bush administration was focused entirely on Iraq. The tenor of the questions from my Latin American visitors was: "You Americans are ignoring us, you don't care about us, you are insulting us by not paying attention, we need you here to help us with our problems, what is wrong with Washington?"

So there is an element of 'darned if you do, darned if you don't' for US foreign policy. On the other hand, George W. Bush's foreign policy was a debacle. There is just no other way to say it. It was poorly thought out. It rested on foolish assumptions about the way the world works, and it is going to take a long time to dig ourselves out. There are a bunch of issues he could have made some progress on, particularly because he is a Republican, and he chose not to. We shall see.

Q: "The lesson of Iraq, then, was that when you lead badly, few follow." *This seems to imply that as long as the United States leads well, it has every right to do so – or is this reading too much into it?*

L: No, I don't think so. There is a tradition of American leadership. As much as Europeans might complain about Americans making the wrong choices, or not doing things the right way – as Churchill said: "You can trust the Americans to do the right thing, but only after they try all the bad things first" – there is an expectation of American leadership. But at the end of the day, leadership implies followership. If people don't believe in where you are going, or they don't want to go where you want to take them, or they don't believe you know how to get them there, or they don't trust you, they are not going to follow.

What Americans don't understand is this: The Bush administration thought that the Germans would moan and grunt, but eventually they would come around because events would prove us right. And what the administration discovered was: This was not like during the Cold War where your allies might swallow their concerns because they were worried about the threat from the Soviet Union, and they needed the Americans to protect them. Events didn't bear the administration out. The United States didn't find weapons of mass destruction. Much of the Bush administration's analysis on how far they could push the envelope by busting other people's chops was that at the end of the day, they would find all these weapons. And everyone would say: "You were right. We Europeans were like the townsfolk in *High Noon*, we knew there was a threat out there, but we didn't have the guts to admit there was one. Thankfully, somebody stood tall and protected us."

In many ways, *High Noon* is the intellectual referent for the Bush administration, and its mental map of how the world works. Instead what happened was that the town gets shot up, and the townsfolk looked at the Gary-Cooper-figure and said: "What the heck did you do?"

Let's face it: The United States is never going to be liked by everybody at the same moment. There is always going to be some kind of anti-Americanism. But the Bush administration has done a lot of things to make that a lot worse. In a world in which we are dealing with solid democracies, you have choices. If you alienate their publics, you either make it harder for their leaders to work with you – because they are afraid of being called George W. Bush's poodle – or you create openings for opposition parties to get into power by running against you. This is how democratic politics works so there is no sense in getting morally outraged by it. On that level, for all of its pedigree and experience, the Bush administration was remarkably naïve. The terrain had changed. This wasn't like dealing with the Soviet Union where when Brezhnev said "I am going to do it," he did it. One of the problems of being a superpower is that you develop bad habits, and you don't recognize how the world has changed.

Q: In your book, you detect "a strategic, but also a moral imperative" in the Bush strategy. How do you evaluate the discussion of morality in politics? Is it the task of an authority somewhat outside the realm of everyday politics to watch over the moral aspects of governing?

L: It is impossible for policy makers to avoid assessing the moral implications of the choices they make. As a result, it is impossible for analysts writing about foreign policy choices to avoid confronting moral considerations. That doesn't mean that those moral calculations are easy to make, in part because there are a multitude of different moral codes. Some people are consequentialists – you judge the means by the ends. Other people are absolutists – there are certain means that are simply forbidden, regardless of what ends they might produce. Beyond that you have all kinds of complexities about trying to assess what the likely consequences of your action are so you can even apply a moral code.

Certainly moral claims were always embedded in the Bush administration's policy. It began with the notion that America was a uniquely just great power and others recognized it as such because we had historically done the right thing rather than the self-interested thing. That gave us a certain moral claim to act that others didn't have. That heavily guided the administration's thinking. You can describe that mindset less charitably, I suppose, but I don't think it is necessarily peculiar to either the Bush administration or to Americans. Many governments and policy makers of whatever nationality can sound very moralistic when they are talking about Darfur, or climate change, or protecting the family. That tends to be fairly common, or at least not limited to Americans.

In terms of being an intellectual and writing about America's role in the world, and writing about choices, at the end of the day you have to come to grips with the moral consequences of the choices that administrations make. In the United States, much of our self-image, our description of ourselves and what America does in the world, comes back to this notion that the United States isn't like other countries: For the most part, it doesn't act simply to advance narrow interests. We are not Russia. We are not China. We stand up for a broader array of principles. But you have to have that moral reckoning.

Q: As for that moral reckoning, should public intellectuals hold the government accountable on behalf of the public?

L: Public intellectuals don't have any particular standing with the broader public. The judgment is going to be made by the voters. The problem is that the voters don't get to have a choice until the next election even if the administration does a messy thing.

What you do as a Senior Fellow at Brookings, or the Council on Foreign Relations, or the Heritage Foundation, is to try to contribute to the debate about what's good and what's bad. There are hundreds, probably thousands of people throwing things against the wall, shouting out ideas, hoping at some point their idea will catch on. That it will stick. Maybe it will persuade other people. Maybe it will become groundswell. This is what the Conservatives did in the 1990s, talking about American weakness, the Clinton administration not having foreign policy priorities, us being a cork bobbing in the current of history. You had all of these conservative thinkers talking to each other, and this harmony emerged about the nature of the world, and what needed to be done.

That is one way to influence thinking. Another way to do things is that you get one person. Maybe the right policy makers will like what you wrote, and they adopt it and become your spokesperson. But ultimately, judgments as to what's good and what's bad are going to be made by voters.

Q: Professor Lindsay, thank you very much for your time.

L: You are very welcome.

Michael Novak

George Frederick Jewett Scholar in Religion, Philosophy, and Public Policy
American Enterprise Institute for Public Policy Research, Washington, D.C.

Q: Mr. Novak, what audience do you have in mind for your publications?

N: I write for many different publications, and I tried to learn different styles ever since I was young. From newspapers to popular magazines to heavier magazines, like *Commentary* or *First Things, National Interest,* and those magazines.

But from the time when I was very young, when I was a graduate student at Harvard, I told one of my professors that I believed a philosopher should be able to sit on a box in a general store and talk to people there, and if you couldn't, you weren't a very good philosopher. He was horrified because he thought philosophy is a very recognized discipline, and there is some truth to it. But my view is: Philosophy is love of man, and you better know about man and the different ranges. And if you come up with something new, there "must be something wrong with it." But it is not as easy as it sounds. So I do try to address a larger public than academic for sure. But I especially have in mind doctors, and lawyers, and journalists. I write about people who are not educated and don't have book-learning. And I think I pay more attention to that than most philosophers, and most professors and journalists. But none of my books have been popular bestsellers or anything like that, I write at too high a level for that. But it is not quite academic writing. It is enough to have some respect in the academy, but it is not the way academicians write.

Q: Do you intend to educate the public? Is it one of your aims to see to it that there are informed, knowledgeable citizens in the United States who will then become qualified members of democracy?

N: I admired as a writer the writings of John Locke. They are very commonsensical, they are demanding – my uncle is not going to read them –

but still they are laid out for the common, he is not writing for Oxford. And Reinhold Niebuhr who probably is America's greatest theologian. He set the pattern. And Jacques Maritain, the French ambassador and Vatican philosopher who had a lot to do with the Universal Declaration of Human Rights he helped formulate. Those sorts of people always believed that 'Ideas have Consequences', to use the slogan. And that the fundamental battle is a battle of ideas. Behind every politic, there is at least one philosophy, sometimes more than one. And when human beings form a distorted image of themselves, when they don't see their own possibilities, and their own weaknesses, they make very bad mistakes in organizing society. So there is a direct connection between thinking clearly and politics. But it isn't immediate, it sometimes works at a distance of a generation or two.

Q: The question came to mind because of a quote I found in the chapter 'How the Catholic church came to terms with democracy', where you say: "To the extent that democracy depends upon the will of the people, it also depends upon the quality of their information and their ability to hear contrasting arguments, well and thoroughly presented."

N: That's right, yes, that is a fair reading. I have learned as I have gotten older how delayed the effect of something can be. Even if some people become convinced of it right away, they are not in a position to do very much with it. But it is good to get those ideas in the public square, and they get people thinking in new ways, and that is very helpful. It loosens up the ground, so it is not too frozen.

Q: Why did you choose foreign politics as one area to focus upon?

N: Because in my lifetime, I had to learn a lot of geography, just to follow what Americans were doing. I didn't know anything about Vietnam, I had to learn, I didn't know anything about Iraq, I had to learn, Kosovo, you name it. If there is a problem in the world, they are going to call Americans. America is the firehouse. Whether that is good or bad, that is the only thing that will do it right now.

And then also my father: When I was seven or eight, World War II was just beginning, September '39, I remember. And he sat me down and said: "This is going to have a tremendous effect on your future." And then later he said: "Read all you can about Fascism and Communism. These are going to be very big ideas for the rest of this century." I didn't know about the end in this century, but he was right. And so, just as a matter of breeding, I began to think that way. And in the United States, when minds changed about what could be done about the unjust situation of Blacks, events started to change – I don't know which came first, maybe you had to have the events awakening the minds, some mix. But you need both together. If they don't walk in step, nothing happens. People put out the noise, and just go on. A friend of mine in Europe, a woman journalist, told me that she thought the most hopeful thing in her lifetime was the Civil Rights Movement in the United States and the progress of Blacks between 1940 and the present. Obama would not have been conceivable – barely – before then.

Q: Maybe public intellectuals are among those who are 'awakening the minds' as well. How would you define the term 'public intellectual'? Does it still point to something relevant these days?

N: Yes. For example, Norman Podhoretz who is the editor of *Commentary* and I think one of the most powerful influences on American thinking in the last twenty years, not the only one, but one of them. He does not write for an academic audience, and saying he is an academic would not be appropriate for him, even though I think he has a doctorate in literature. But he certainly expresses ideas at a quite fundamental level, explicitly facing the philosophy and anthropology involved and finding his way to a moral vision – he wasn't there at the beginning – large enough to handle complex questions.

So that's what I think an intellectual is. Academics have become so much more specialized. They read each other, and they talk to their little world. That is the reason why there are places like AEI, The Brookings Institution, there are hundreds of think tanks now, there didn't use to be. The people in politics, and even in business, are too busy to be worried about ideas. The people in the academy are too box-nest specialized, so there is really a lot of room for people who think about where the country should be ten years from now. Or what's going to happen when this happens? We have a law for licensing radio and television stations, assigning airwaves and so on. And that law was due to expire in 1992 or so. So when I came here at the AEI, we already had programs going, what should happen? And if you think through what should happen, you can be a big assistance when the time comes.

Q: Is the think tank the best solution between academia and the government?

N: I think it is a very good one, and I would say for me, but I don't think it is merely personal. It is certainly the best one for me. With one exception: If I were in the university and I had to be training graduate students, I would increase the force of ideas, and I miss that a lot. So that's the price you pay. But I know it is not just for me because more and more academics want to come to a think tank. They are tired of the academic politics and – if I may say so – the triviality of much of what is done there. So from a very early age, I have prepared myself for involvement in the public questions, from my very first writings you can see this. And that is partly for the influence of Niebuhr, Maritain, and some others that I liked, like Charles Péguy.

Q: The latter two were European thinkers. When we cross the Atlantic, the situation of intellectuals seems to be slightly different. American intellectuals seem to have lived with a certain tension from the beginning: A claim to speak from a distanced, somewhat 'disinterested' position, and at the same time, a claim to act upon and from within society. What do you make of this tension?

N: I disagree with both parts of your statement. I don't think disinterestedness is an ideal that human beings appropriately can work for. It's good enough if you are an instrument, a telescope or something.

But what I think we need to work hard yet is largeness of mind so you can understand what other parties are saying, and see why they are saying it. You can walk a little while in the moccasins of the other one, and then you can get a conversation that is reasonably decent. It takes a lot of work and patience. But if you just propound from your side, and demean the other side – too much of American politics is that way. Hurling names at the other side, it doesn't get you anywhere. So I don't think disinterestedness, but large-mindedness is crucial. "ACU-science students, take the views of the person you most disagree with, and articulate them and defend them. You don't have to believe it, just show me that you really understand from the other side. If you are an atheist, take the view of the believer, and show me. If you are a believer, take the view of the atheist, and show me." Like that.

As for the other part, the will to intervene, it might be the case a little bit. Here is the way the American Enterprise Institute is set up. We are set up to do long-range work – in that sense more like a university. If you want to know what policies the Congress should be arguing about next week, and what the background is, you go to Heritage. They will tell you. It is down and dirty. You don't have time to do everything, you get the best you can, and it is very good, but it is not what we do. We are a bit more interested in problems that haven't emerged yet, or that will emerge. I think of us as more like explorers, trying to feel the practical constraints, but trying to explore what possible answers there are. And there is no point in us being partisan. What's important is to be right, to get it exactly. You can't hit that always, but you have got to keep aiming at that. I work as good as nobody unless we get it right, unless we are accurate.

A friend's daughter worked for a summer writing preparatory notes for Senator Bradley, who was one of our more liberal, but very intelligent. She was preparing his little briefing books that he'd take everywhere he went. What he wanted to know was: "What are the strongest arguments for my position? What are the strongest arguments for the other side? What are some arguments I haven't heard? And then I want to know the answers to questions." And she said she found that pamphlets and articles from the American Enterprise Institute were the most useful to her because they really helped her to frame the argument. When we are at our best, that is what we are trying to do. We generally try to work with somebody from the Left, and we always keep people here who are pretty much from the Left: Norman J. Ornstein, who is the most-quoted man in America – we call him 'Quotestein' – because his specialty is the Congress and you really can't write about the Congress unless you talk to Norman. Bill Schneider was here, Ben J. Wattenberg is just retired. I was a Democrat when I came here. I am still a Democrat, but I can't vote for them anymore. I just don't think they get it. You know what a Neoconservative is? A Neoconservative is a progressive with two teenaged daughters, said to begin to see some things.

Q: You say in your book that you prefer the term 'Whigs'?

N: Yes, because I didn't like it when we were called 'Neoconservatives' because that was coming from Michael Harrington, a socialist, a social democrat. That was a put-down, you couldn't call anybody worse than a Conservative. And to say 'Neoconservative' is like saying 'Pseudo-Conservative'. It was a put-down. But the term got to be used, and it is still used, and there is no use fighting it. But if I am allowed to introduce the terms, I mean somebody who believes in the tradition of liberty, but believes also in the importance of tradition, and the tacit, and the silent. So I prefer 'Whig'. The other thing I like about 'Whig' is that it makes people think because they don't know what you mean. With 'Neoconservative', it has changed completely since the war, over the last five years, to mean foreign-policy hawks. And 'Neoconservative' again became a way of putting it down. And it was a way that was inevitably described as Jewish, and by no means 'Neoconservative' is Jewish. So it had a little anti-Semitic tinge, and purposefully, too.

So I don't think you can be disinterested, and I do think ideas have a long-term influence. So we are wrestling to get things right. What is the right name to call our enemy in Iraq? My friend George Weigel has just written a little book which is very good on the Jihadists, and that is where he pushes. I don't like it myself. He doesn't like my word, I don't like his. But that's what we need, we need an argument about that.

Q: Intellectuals have repeatedly been portrayed as rather secular authorities – how do you reconcile religiousness, faith, and the maxims of reason? You begin your epilogue by saying: "Many intellectuals look at the world in purely secular terms. This is good as far as it goes, and yet its internal design does not allow it to go very far."

N: Well, you have to remember here that when you are talking about faith, you are talking about the Jewish and Christian faith which understands God in terms of *logos* or mind, or insight, really, which I think is the best word for logos. Theology, sociology, it is all based on *logos*. So it is a particular vision of God. It is different from the Islamic in that the Jewish and Christian God stresses intellect and understanding. Intellect in the sense of understanding, not intellect in the sense of logic or geometry. And therefore the God of particulars who can have a favorite people, Israel. It is a particular kind of God. He knows the 'lily in the field' – I am just picking out some text –, so he knows the particulars. That is a particular kind of faith, but as you can see, it is not contrary to reason. In fact it is one of the great justifications for reason. And I have been very struck by the number of historians and scientists who began to see that Judaism and Christianity gave a tremendous impulse to inquiry, knowledge, universities – because it is crucial of their way of understanding the world. If a creator made all this, it is filled with intelligence, and we should be able to discover it if we use our heads. It takes patience and time and aestheticism, and you have to sit on your veranda a lot, read in the dark, write or type. It is hard work, but it is what human beings ought to do. It is how you imitate God, it is how you take advantage of the creation as God made it, try to improve it.

The other thing is: Secular thinkers for the last three hundred years – not all, but the predominant movement – have been very anti-religious: the Voltaire-side. That is true in Britain, more true on the continent. "*Écrasez l'infâme!*" But they really do miss a lot of reality. The German philosopher Habermas – some people describe him as the most important public philosopher; he is not the smartest, or the most learned, but he is certainly very public – wrote after September 11 that it just changed his picture of the world. He had thought secularism was the cutting edge, and he suddenly realized that atheism and secularism are just little islands in the midst of a vast ocean. And it is a very turbulent ocean, and it is getting bigger.

When I came to Washington in 1978, nobody knew what to do with a theologian in a think tank. It never happened. They went off when I wanted to say 'Grace' before meals. But then Jimmy Carter had come along as a born-again Christian. No well-educated journalist knew what a born-again Christian is. They just didn't know. So my phone started ringing. And then Iran erupted. I mean, this is one religious problem after another. So AEI had a competitive advantage, now other think tanks have theologians, too. It is just the dimension of life you have got to cope with, like it or not. And I noticed even the atheists, C.R. Dawkins and Christopher Hitchens and so forth, are really defensive. Those books are cries of pain in my view. They feel very lonely. And they feel like they are spitting in the wind. No matter how they argue, people won't listen to them, particularly in the United States. And they are only expected to change. So Hitchens ends up saying: There is something permanent that we are vivifying about religion, but we still have got to attack it, we have got to keep it under control. It is just an important dimension in life, and it turns out to be extremely influential in politics. The man who brought me here, William J. Baroody, with roots in Lebanon, he knew how important religion is to democracy in Lebanon. He knew that religion was the cutting edge of the differences. You can argue whatever you want, you might say it is power, money, whatever. But people do very irrational things sometimes just because of religion. So he brought me here to make this better known in this country. I think it is very important, and very dynamic, and

I believe the world will probably be more religious in fifty years than it is now. The question is what sort of religion.

Q: What does your readership expect from you: Concrete policy proposals, or a visionary framework for their nation's course in the world?

N: You should have a visionary frame because politics is like a story, a narrative. And you imagine the way history is going to go, or should go. So it is like telling a story. Now you have to have somebody to flesh out what the story is and what the implications are, what you are missing, and where it might go wrong. So you should be working toward it, but especially in America it has to be a rather practical vision. Jacques Maritain called it 'the practical practical', that is it is not just practical philosophy the way Aristotle has said. It is really thinking about specific policies. A welfare reform – given what you know about human nature, what are the likely consequences going to be? And when you do that, it is very helpful. But that is not the biggest thing you need to do. The biggest thing is to keep looking with fresh eyes on things to see what's working, what is not. If you have a vision of what human beings ought to be – what Lincoln called 'the better angels of our nature', and also the worse angels of our nature – you try to think, at least I do, what are we missing at this moment in history? You no sooner think you are on the right track when the world changes.

Q: Even though it brings forward what you call a 'rather practical' vision, your book seems to have an all-encompassing, idealistic appeal. Is it time one tried to create a unifying myth for America, especially since 2001?

N: It is not just since 2001, although that helped. 2001 brought us together for a year or two, very powerful.

The consensus in this country for fifty or sixty years was: We have to have our own version of the welfare state. Not quite social-democratic as in Germany or France, but still they became sort of ideals. There were a number of books written when I was going to university and graduate school: "There are no Conservatives in America! There are a few cranks!" The only thing you could be in America is a Liberal, by which they meant a democratic socialist. They completely changed the meaning of the word 'liberal' in the 1930s. 'Liberal' used to mean 'free from the state', that is what you are liberated from. Beginning in the 1930s under

John Dewey, Liberals began to define themselves in the terms of using the state as an instrument to make the world better. The more you do that, the more you begin to imitate Europe. We had two or three centuries of being the New World different from Europe, and for the first time we had an elite which looked to Europe for leadership. What they were failing to notice is that many of the ideas they picked up don't work, at least not here. The welfare state is going to destroy itself because it promises so many benefits, and it will never be able to pay for them. And the demography is such that we are having fewer young people, and that is partly because the state taxes so heavily that people don't have the space to have another child. And that is what we need, three at least in every family.

My view is that people on the Left – as I was – feel out on a limb and the branch being sawed off. And there is real desperation there. Then people on the Left tend to think that people on the Right are stupid. Well, they really think we are evil. Evil and stupid. It was so humiliating to them to lose to George W. Bush twice, both elections they should have won easily. They just can't believe it. So they invent demons to explain it, completely divorced from reality. That has really embittered our politics. It is the competition over some big ideas, and the wheel has turned. But many on the Left don't get it. That is what Obama represents: The last gasp, or at least a big gasp. He talks as if the state universal health care is going to solve it all. I think it is going to do great damage to a very good health system and it is going to create financial burdens the country won't be able to sustain.

Q: Who – in your opinion – should watch over the moral aspects of politics? What does morality mean in the context of politics?

N: Blaise Pascal wrote: "The first moral obligation is to think clearly," and that means to take responsibility for the consequences of your own actions. And that is how you have to think in a moment of passion. You have to think clearly about what the likely consequences are, including consequences you won't be able to predict. Somebody has to play that role. In other words, I want to extend the notion of morality from what you are saying. I don't mean the dress codes, and sex codes, and the movies. Péguy again: "Everything begins with *la mystique* and ends with *la politique*." There is a truth in that. You have to get the vision and then you have to realize it in flesh and blood: the *politique*. And then it becomes bureaucratized and instrumentalized and people no longer believe in it, and you need a new beginning. We are going through several of those at once. One globally, politically, and one economically, and I suppose morally as well – certainly with Communism and now with Jihadism.

And then we also have this contestation of ideas in America. Barack Obama really thinks, and Hillary Clinton sometimes agrees with him – though I know she doesn't think this – that if they tax the top one or two percent more, it will be more fair. They don't seem to grasp the fact that the top one percent pays forty percent of all the income that the government receives through income taxes. So if they tax them more, they are going to try to make less income, they will take it in other ways than income. It is just the way human incentives work. It is not evil. For instance, when I began to write and lecture more – 37 years ago – and to get a sufficient income from that, I thought it would be wise to incorporate because the corporation paid much lower taxes: 15 percent tax rate compared to the individual. Then when they changed the income tax to come way down, from 70 to 50 to 30, more and more people thought: Why go through all the trouble of a corporation? And they began just taking this income. That is what made the wealth of the wealthy seem bigger than it was. It is the same income, now declared differently. I just do not understand how people on the Left haven't learnt that. I had to learn it in the early 1980s, I didn't believe that or know it. Everything I have seen so far confirms it.

Q: Let's talk a little bit more about the importance of ethics, values, and virtues in your work. To quote from the epilogue: "Considering the large number of sound habits necessary in the political, economic, and cultural spheres of the free society, it is obvious that the free society must also become an unusually virtuous society." What role exactly do ethical questions play in American democracy today?

N: First of all, I prefer to analyze in terms of virtues because that means it is something you and I can do concrete and real. If you have a really bad temper, and you gain some control over it, that is power. You now can do things you couldn't do before. George Washington was like that. He had a horrible temper as a young man. He learned to master it so much that when he was finally general, people were amazed at his equanimity. And he needed it because he kept losing battles. He had to keep an even keel. I prefer that to the term that is coming to vogue in the last forty years, values. Because values is Nietzsche's term. When you don't have any values, when nihilism is the truth, and you just choose to do this, and I just choose to do that, it is preferences. I value this, you value that. There is no real argument in between, there is no intellectual content. It is will. You will, I will. I think that is a recipe for fascism, for totalitarianism. And the people who have the strongest will will prevail. I don't like to use the word values. I think when you say values, you are surrendering the issue. Virtues is harder, but look: Latin America countries have had several chances to become capitalist, democratic societies. They are just too much taking advantage in cheating. People are not honest. And then other people resent it.

I will give you another example: In Poland, after the fall of Communism, people your age and a little bit older began to look around what they could do now that they could. So they would drive their little cars into East Germany, buy fresh vegetables, drive back to Poland and sell them, because they weren't available yet. By their own initiative, they made the economy move. There were 500.000 new entrepreneurs in Poland in the first year, and 500.000 new ones in the second year. But what they learned is if you are going to do it, you have to work much harder, you have to stay up much later. And you have to take the down-turns and the bad news as well as the good news and the up-turns. It requires a different character. Older people who were accustomed to having all the big decisions of their lives made for them by the state didn't like the new system. It frightened them. They didn't know what to do.

I concluded from this: Liberty – meaning democracy, and personal initiative in economic life – requires more virtues, a different kind of habits, a different structure than socialist habits. The Japanese are so terrific. They are so disciplined and so well-organized and so intelligent about how they do things. They are such a small population with no natural resources, not even energy. They produce ten percent of everything produced in the world. It is a triumph of the human spirit, really, the human ability to organize. It is the habits they have taught one another for the last 150 years. I think a lot rides on the habits you teach. And the kind of habits you teach gives your culture a certain character.

Q: Who does the teaching? Who should be in charge?

N: That is what's broken down. Until 1940, families did it. And your local newspaper did it. And your local pastor did it. And your local schoolteacher did it. And they were all working in harmony. In this country, it was very heavily biblical, even though the schools were non-confessional. They would begin with a prayer, examples were taken from biblical life. Abraham did this, Moses did this, or whatever. But then the rise of newspapers began to disturb that because some of the newspapers were in New York and Los Angeles, and they began to spread across. And radio began to create a national sense. And television advented. So we lost the normal roots of our vision. We gained new competitors for that vision coming through the little family shrine in the living room with the burning light.

Look, if you are bringing up a fifteen-year old daughter in the time of Madonna, and Madonna tells her one thing, and her father who is an old geek tells her another thing, who is she going to listen to? There is a new form of moral instruction right in your own home. That paved the way for an intellectual class, the class of the communicators – what Margaret Thatcher called the 'chattering classes': People who talk and present the ideas on television and the newspapers and the movies that supplant the teachings of the olders. That has been a big transformation. It is when things break down more that people say: Wait a minute, we have got to think this through again.

Q: What about the very recent past, the time since September 11: Has the authority of the intellectual class increased?

N: Their capacity for mischief has increased. Their monopoly has been broken because Conservatives have discovered that their audience likes radio, partly because it is more various. Every state has its own talk show host and they know their state, so they keep close to the people. Whereas television is this national class, they all went to Harvard and Yale. You get the picture. And they are terribly afraid of one of those eyebrows. The power of the raised eyebrow is the most powerful instrument in the world. And if they write or present a show on something that bothers their peers, it bothers them. So there is a powerful principle of conformity. Senator Eugene J. McCarthy used to say that it is like birds in the fall, coming in a big flock. They all land on a telegraph wire. And then one of them leaves, and they all leave. That is the way journalists are. There is a certain truth in that. That monopoly has been broken up because the radios have become more powerful. Nobody on television commands twenty million people in the way that Rush Limbaugh commands them, he has that big an audience. And then Fox News and some other cable news have created more variety. It is not just ABC, CBS, NBC, and PBS. It is a little bit more lively than that. Now it is like six to one. Against one. But just seeing Fox is a refreshment. You are going to hate it, but it gives a different view. And if you attend closely, it will help you understand the other side better. What is called the cultural war means there is a contestation: Who are we Americans? What should we think of ourselves, which way should we go? Right now, there is a big battle over that.

Q: Since September 11, has this battle become even bigger? Does the public have a certain demand for a guiding voice of reason that will explain to them their nation's course in the world?

N: I think it is older than September 11. I think it goes back to approximately 1965 when the paperbacks were invented. Kennedy helped turn the romance of American intellectuals and professors and young people to politics. When I was graduating, politics was a disreputable occupation. Nobody would want their child to be a politician. It meant somebody who not exactly lies, but never tells the truth, always says what you want to hear, and who is friends with everybody. Just not a nice kind of person. Kennedy changed that. There was a distinct change then. From then on, the intellectuals had become more romantic about getting into politics, becoming speech writers, writing position papers, having an hour with the candidate.

That has changed, but it precedes September 11. September 11 quieted it for a while. The sheer sight of American fire trucks with the American flag flying going down the streets of Manhattan and thousands of people cheering it really intimidated the anti-war Left. Before there was a war, they were anti-war. But they had to keep silent. They were afraid of making spectacles of themselves, most of them. Most of the Democrats voted for the war. It was very funny, it is just an odd political thing, but I loved it: During the summer before the war in Iraq, 2002, Dick Cheney said in a speech that of course the administration did not have to go to Congress because of the war powers inherent in the Constitution. And they didn't invent a declaration of war. There was a huge uproar. And then the president said something like that, and another huge uproar. So we spent the month of May, June, July arguing that no, they couldn't do it alone, they had to go to Congress. So in August, the president says: "OK, we are going to Congress." Now there is an election coming up in November! So the Democrats got their wish, but now they were stuck and they voted overwhelmingly for the war which most of them probably didn't like. We have a saying in American Football called a 'Mousetrap Play'. You have seven men on the line. You move one of your men this way, behind the center, and it leaves a hole. And you deliberately let the other guy charge in. And then when he is past you, you run right through. Bring them in and snap the trap shut. That is Bush's favorite play. He does that all the time. He sets up the press when the Democrats run away. And they always fall for it.

Q: Despite all the disagreement and the ensuing argument you just described, is there a general consensus across political affiliations regarding foreign policy, i.e. the American version of democracy should be disseminated throughout the world? If anything, the discussion centers around the most effective way to do that?

N: I think that was the case. But since the Vietnam War, that has broken down because there were a lot of people on the Left who suddenly realized to protect the welfare state – which is what they are really interested in – they can't have a robust defense policy. That is too costly. The people won't allow themselves to be taxed above a certain limit. I think there comes to be an anti-overseas involvement party – what George McGovern, the 1972 candidate, called "Come home, America." That is an old tendency in America, 'fortress America', no foreign entanglements. And if you live in most of America, why would you get involved in the world? It is so peaceful, beautiful fields, fishing streams, and mountains.

Q: Is that where it is going again?

N: That is where a certain element of the Democratic Party is going. And they have long roots in that. They were the ones who opposed Lincoln in the Civil War. Why was Lincoln causing so much trouble? 'Just let them have slavery'.

All I want to say is, things have changed since Vietnam, or were occasioned by Vietnam. So there is a really deep emotional split, an ideas split between the two parties now. And it has been fomented. And the Democrats have lost so many elections, seven of the last eight or nine. They should have won half of those that they lost. So they are really angry, and frustrated, and bitter, and mean. Bush is a war criminal, Cheney is the Evil Empire incarnate. It is bizarre. That is what is meant by the culture wars.

The other really deep issue in American life is abortion. Some women have decided – I think it is a minority of women, but it is a good number – that their liberty depends on the right to an abortion. And they will have no surrender or weakening on that principle. But meanwhile, to do that, they have to cover up the reality of abortion. They don't want any pictures of abortion on television. They don't want any discussion of what it is: To abort is just another word for to kill. To take the life off. And they don't want to say that. So there is a systematic pattern of lies. The great unspoken divide between the parties is abortion. Now the Democrats have begun to recognize that and they are promoting a number of pro-life Democrats. That is how they got their majority. Ten or twelve of their victories last time were from pro-life candidates. The Democratic Party used to be very strongly pro-life. It has changed since the last government period.

The Democratic Party was the party that had the will to fight World War II and took responsibility for it, and did it well. A lot of mistakes, but then every war is filled with mistakes. Truman really resisted Communism. I just read a letter today in *First Things*, a letter to the editors which argues that nowadays we can't count on a consensus. There is a family of principles, there are family resemblances, but they are not all the same. So you have to make three or four arguments at once to meet this group, and that group, and that group. And that seems to me more true.

Q: Does this also hold for foreign politics these days?

N: Yes.

Q: All the more so?

N: Well, foreign policy less than war. But even foreign policy insofar as free trade is foreign policy. Certain people are putting great pressure on free trade, and they are crazy. It is an ideological cry of the Left. They think that is what working people want. It is not true. Working people in certain industries benefit by that because we are the ones selling the exports.

Q: How important is it that the United States remains the only superpower in the world? You mentioned recent isolationist tendencies?

N: Superpower isn't good. It is a dangerous position to be in. Power corrupts. It would be better for us, it would be hard, but when China and Russia grew more. Better and more dangerous in another way, but anyway.

I do think that the world really needs the United States. We settled Kosovo for Europe. It is Europe's problem, and the Europeans couldn't agree what to do. They said, we'll do fifty percent, and you'll do fifty percent. We ended up doing 95 percent. It is just the way the world is. Europe cannot afford to do much outside of Europe that has risk and deficits with it. It can give foreign aid. So I think the United States should remain engaged in the world. Human dignity, human people need it. In Africa, if we didn't put thirty billion dollars in there for AIDS and have tremendous success, who would do it?

Q: This difference between the United States and Europe as you describe it, does it come down to differing mindsets? Or is it because of the sheer military power the United States has?

N: Europe has enjoyed an unprecedented prosperity since about 1960. And the fact that poor Europeans at your grandparents' age can now get into their little VWs or whatever cars they have and drive on beautiful roads to the Riviera and eat marvelous food and not worry about war or anything – it is such a wonderful era, and I don't blame Europeans for enjoying it, especially after the early part of the 20th century when Europeans suffered so much.

In addition, European families are very small. It is much harder to send your son to war when he is the only one. In the old days, people had five or six children, and it was almost expected that one or two would join the army. It was a good way up. But things were changing. I noticed that after a wave of fifteen or twenty years of anti-Americanism, exacerbated but not caused by the Iraq War, Sarkozy gets elected on a pattern of loving America, and Merkel, and Berlusconi. I think people who focus on the future of liberty and the threats to it are going to find common alliance between Europe and the United States. I just hope they will be faster than the people who don't want to know the sacrifices, because it is going to take sacrifices to do it. That is what I think the underline is. I am rather hopeful about the trends.

Q: This reminds me of Robert Kagan's thesis that Americans might be quicker in perceiving threats than Europeans simply because they have the means to meet these threats. For him, Europeans tend to downplay certain threats in order not to get engaged because they lack the means.

N: Yes, but that is deliberate. It is only in the last forty years because until World War II Europeans had the military power way ahead of the United States. We were a very, very weak country in military power. That is why Hitler did his miscalculation. He thought America is a paper tiger. What it was, but we had the capacity then to move out of it very quickly.

But since World War II Europe has had this amazing prosperity, a middle-class the first time for most people. They don't want it disturbed. It has been so nice, and it is so rare in history that it has happened. I don't blame them a bit. But the truth is they don't want to build up their armies. They don't want to have even a sufficient defense force for Europe, let alone a distant defense. We had a talk here from the Polish ambassador to Iraq, a former general in the Polish army in Iraq, and he was saying: "The Polish soldiers in Iraq are the furthest Poles have been from the borders of Poland for four hundred years. But I can tell you: Myself and my men and many others think we'd rather defend Poland in Baghdad than on the borders of the river with Russia." But again I think Europeans – even intelligent, sensitive, well-meaning-toward-America Europeans – tremble at the expense involved, and the risk involved. And they can't help just wishing America would do it and keep quiet about it.

Q: So the world is better off with the way America is engaged in it right now?

N: If you took a poll of people in the field of theology, even thirty years ago when one was done, a majority said: "No! America is a force for evil in the world rather than good." A left-wing way of thinking about these things was spread, especially in theology. But I don't understand that. I mentioned AIDS in Africa. Without United States investment and help and ideas and so forth, China and India would not have been able to take half a billion people out of poverty in the last twenty years. It is the biggest jump out of poverty, a great leap forward. But it didn't come from Communism, it came from capitalism. I think that is a good thing, even if China turns out to be a problem down the line.

And I think Jihadism is a powerful international force. The only way I see to end it: The people in the Middle East – it is not all Muslims –, the Arabs have been among the most persecuted people in the world with the least defense of their own dignity and their own minds. Their own governments don't do it, the religious police don't do it. Nobody ever speaks up for them. So there is no opportunity for young men. Even if you go to Hamburg and get your degree, what are you going to do? There are no jobs in Saudi-Arabia for you. And if they have them, they would rather give them to a German, or an Italian with a little more caché. So what are they going to do with all that energy? And all that sexual energy? Therefore I believe underlying you have got to start a democratic movement in the Arab countries. And if you succeed, then there is an option. You don't have to go to violence, you can watch a country move ahead without turning to violence. That is what we are attempting. It may be foolhardy, it may not be able to work. But I think it is the only long-term way to do it. The other way to look at it is you have to have a fire-brigade so when there is an outbreak, you can act. I don't think we'll be able to keep up with it. There will be too many fires.

Q: Mr. Novak, thanks a lot for your time.

N: You are very welcome.

Joseph S. Nye, Jr.

University Distinguished Service Professor
Sultan of Oman Professor of International Relations
John F. Kennedy School of Government
Harvard University, MA

Q: Professor Nye, what audience do you have in mind for your publications?

N: I write different things for different audiences. When I write for political scientists in political science journals, I write for a relatively narrow audience. As an academic, you have to do a certain amount of that to pay your dues. You don't start out as a public intellectual, you start out writing academic articles in academic journals, with lots of footnotes, using the jargon of the profession. But if you are interested in reaching a broader audience, you have to communicate in a more accessible language, and you have to put your ideas in a form which as I sometimes say my mother could understand. My mother is very smart, but she is not interested in political science. So a book like *Soft Power* is written to appeal to a broader audience, but let's face it, it is still not a popular audience. It is people who read the *New York Times*, or *Wall Street Journal*, but it is not people who read *USA Today* or who don't read any newspapers at all.

So there is a spectrum of journals, and a spectrum of audiences, and what I am trying to do is write for a part of that spectrum that is serious and wants to listen to an argument. But the argument expressed in language which is readily accessible. So you will find there are several hundred footnotes at the back of this book – if somebody wants to find out what's the basis for that, you can find it out. Whereas if you are writing a newspaper column, there are no footnotes whatsoever. So I aim at the reader who wants accessible argument, but documented if they wanted to pursue the documented. However, I also write a lot of op-eds, newspaper columns which are not documented. I probably write twenty-five of those a year.

Q: You mention newspaper columns. When it comes to op-ed articles, do you have an 'education project' for the American public in mind? Do you try to provide people with a frame of knowledge that will help them become 'concerned' citizens?

N: Yes, I think the reason I would spend the time writing op-eds is because I'd like to have some influence on how people see these major issues. The feeling that you can contribute to the public debate is the incentive. Money involved in op-eds is relatively little, and the time can sometimes be small, but sometimes it will take more time than you'd expect. So the main incentive for doing it is to try to influence the public debate.

Q: How would you define the term 'public intellectual'? Is it still an appropriate term that points to a relevant phenomenon?

N: It is a term which is widely used. And it obviously is somebody who tries to affect the debate on policy issues. But it is always a little bit difficult to say where the cut-off line is. In other words, there are some people who spend all their time on going on television programs, writing op-eds, and so forth, who would be clearly called public intellectuals. There are other scholars who may be writing half a dozen op-eds a year or even fewer, but when they write them, they have a very powerful effect. And then there is others who don't write anything at all. The ones who don't write anything at all are probably not thought of as public intellectuals. But where is the cut-off line? If you take someone like John Rawls, who is a very influential philosopher in theories of Liberalism, I doubt that he wrote many op-eds, or I don't remember seeing them, but his ideas did get into public discourse quite widely, and I think one would think of him as a public intellectual, although he didn't spend that time going on television programs, or writing op-eds. So it is a little bit hard to see where the cut-off line is.

Q: When we look back on history, American intellectuals seem to have lived with a certain tension from the beginning. On the one hand, a need to keep a critical distance from society so as not to lose their outside perspective. On the other hand, an intention to critically intervene in society. What do you make of the claim that they speak from a distanced point of view – given the fact that many intellectuals today are affiliated with universities, the government, or a think tank?

N: Again, there are different public intellectuals. Somebody like Noam Chomsky who is part of MIT makes his reputation academically by being a first-class scholar of linguistics. But his public intellectual role has very little to do with professional linguistics or his institutional base. He is a very vociferous critic of American society and foreign policy. So there is a person who is university-based, who acts as a public intellectual in a field that is not his own. You can think of another person like Paul Krugman who is a distinguished economist but who writes for the *New York Times* on a weekly basis in his own field of political economy. Both of them are public intellectuals, and both of them are university-based, but in very different ways.

Q: Both Chomsky and Krugman have been criticized by Richard Posner who published a 'Study of Decline' regarding American intellectuals. In the tradition of Richard Hofstadter and Zygmunt Bauman, others have joined him in claiming a gradual decline in importance that the intellectual has suffered over the years. Would you say that intellectuals have regained some authority again since September 11?

N: Perhaps. I think it is true that crises can create opportunities in a society where you want a broader leadership. But the idea that public intellectuals have declined because they were in a position of translating the government to the people – I do not think either Chomsky or Krugman fit that description. I think the more important thing is: You are now in the age of information, the age of the Internet. There is a surplus of information, and there is a deficit of attention. And that does not have to do with decline of the public intellectuals along the theories you just mentioned, that is to do with the overload of information channels. Bloggers are now absorbing more and more attention. But there is a market there, and people find the niches in the market that they want, and pay attention to those bloggers. But then there still is a desire to have some reality checks. So they turn to the quality press very often as the places where you can get a reality check about what you have read on the blogs.

So I think there is something in your theory about after 9/11, a sense of crisis, people looking for interpretations that help them. But the theory about the decline of public intellectuals because they are too much caught up by the government, or because they know less about what they are talking about – that doesn't impress me so much. I would look more at who will supply your information.

Q: The last quarter of the 20ᵗʰ century saw many thinkers take a 'post-modern' stance on reality: They substituted their belief in a 'universal truth' for a belief in 'many truths', all of them equally and 'relatively' valid. However, statements made by public intellectuals in their publications – on the state of the nation, on the desired course of foreign policy – do claim a specific validity or truth. How do you reconcile these two claims?

N: In an open market place of ideas the claims will either be accepted or not accepted, depending on the quality of their arguments. There is certainly no shortage of opportunities for competing opinion.

I think the bigger problem is the public sorting itself out into niches. In the past, when you had few broadcast media, and a few major papers, a lot of people listened to things they did not like to listen to. In the age of cable networks and the Internet, the danger is that the public segments itself into a niche, so people listen to the things they want to listen to that reinforce their pre-existent feelings. I think that is a greater danger: That the public becomes fragmented. So the public intellectual may claim an absolute truth. In the past, they might have had that more challenged. Today, it may be just claiming an absolute truth to a bunch of already true believers. And I think it is important to try to overcome that. Yesterday I reviewed two books in the *Washington Post* by John Bolton and Strobe Talbott who have absolutely opposite views on international governance. And I concluded the review by saying you should probably read both of these books, but if you only have time to read one, read the one which you think is going to be more disagreeable as you will learn more. I am afraid that is not often done.

Q: So although people turn to bloggers on the Internet and other easily accessible sources to have their opinion confirmed, public intellectuals still function as a back-up authority? They are still crucial as truth seekers?

N: Can be, yes. Some of those public intellectuals wind up being public intellectuals not for the general public, but for their selected public. I am more worried about the fragmentation of that mind. I reach to the converted. That there be a position that people can read across different ideological preferences. For example, I subscribe to the journal *The Weekly Standard* which I disagree with philosophically, but I subscribe to it because I want to hear the views of people who have an opposite view from mine. Whereas I don't subscribe to liberal journals because I more or less know what they are going to say. But I think it is the other way round. Most subscribers subscribe to what they already believe in.

Q: How would you estimate the balance of power between the academic world and the world of practical politics? Has it changed recently? Why did you choose the position of an academic?

N: I think academics have become more academic over time. And the gap on policy has been filled by think tanks. Within the academic professions, there has grown an increased specialization, an increased emphasis on what was called the guild mentality: People get promoted by relatively narrow focus.

It is harder to do something like Krugman does. Fellow economists scorn that. You actually lose standing in your profession even though you may gain it in a broader public. So I think in that sense the balance has shifted away from academic intellectuals addressing the public, and there is some data that actually support this.

As for my own case, I didn't originally intend to go into academic life. I went to do a Ph.D. and did my work in Africa as I was interested in Africa. But I thought I might go into government. And then Harvard offered me a job teaching. I thought I would try it for a little while. It turned out I liked teaching, and I also liked writing. So I wound up doing it. My early writings, they were primarily academic. After I had established my position as an academic, and when I came back from government, I decided I wanted to reach a broader audience than just the other academics. My personal experience was: I went into academics because I liked teaching and writing. I gradually broadened out with time to address a broader audience.

Q: So you will either be an established academic or a prominent columnist? You will either become a dedicated journalist or gain academic standing?

N: Krugman did that. Krugman proved himself as an academic economist before he did this. If he had started out just writing columns for the *New York Times*, he would not have got the tenure at Princeton or anywhere.

Q: But now that he has tenure...

N: Once you have tenure, you have more freedom to choose what audience you want to write for. But many academic economists do not want to write for a broad public, they want to write for real economists. And their standing as economists: Economists are always very precise about how they rank each other. Their standing is judged by what they write in the *American Economic Review*, not by what they write in the *New York Times*.

Q: Is it actually possible to specialize in academia and at the same time translate what you know to a broad public?

N: It may be harder in some fields than others; in more technical fields, it may be somewhat harder to do that. I think you can do both. But if you don't maintain your academic productivity, and you just turn to op-eds, you are probably going to lose standing.

Foreign Policy had a ranking of the twenty-five leading scholars in international relations two years ago. Of those twenty-five, a large majority did not have government experience and did not write as public intellectuals. I think I got ranked number six, and I had done both academic writing and public writing. It is possible to do it. You might look at that list and judge for yourself as to how many people manage to do both.

Q: What is your opinion on morality in politics? How important is it to keep up moral guidelines in political decisions, and who is supposed to make sure it's being done?

N: Moral judgments are very important but they come from many sources. They come from people in the clergy, they come from editorial writers in the newspapers, they come from everyday people who write letters to the editor, and they can also come from public intellectual writing. But I think it is important if you are both an academic and somebody who is writing for a broader public – moral judgments are important, and important to communicate to the public in a democracy – to be very careful not to let these moral judgments feed back into your academic analysis. The danger is that as you become a preacher, you no longer are an analyst. So keeping those roles separate is important.

Q: Would you agree that there is a general consensus among American intellectuals that their nation's version of democracy should be disseminated across the world, and that controversies arise mainly regarding the most effective way to go about this?

N: Well, there are probably more Americans who think that their form of democracy is the right form than the contrary. And then within that group there are differences on what is the right way to disseminate it. There are some Americans that would feel that democracy will vary by culture, and it is a mistake to try to export a particular form of democracy. John Kennedy got that right when he talked about making the world safe for diversity. I would consider myself more in that second category than in the first category. There are lots of forms of democracy, and there are lots of forms of capitalism.

Q: Kennedy's quote echoes Wilson's famous statement from the early 20th century. If you look back at history, the idea of disseminating American democracy in the world seems to have a long tradition. What about today, though? How important is it that the United States remains the sole superpower?

N: I think there is a distinction between exporting the American style of democracy, and supporting the growth of democracy in other countries. There is a difference between saying that America as a superpower, as the largest power, can create an international order which is more conducive to diversity and democracy as opposed to saying the Americans have to be in control of everything. So I think the first of these two formulations is more important than the second.

Q: How should the United States convey these claims to the rest of the world? To quote from your book: "[T]he new strategy was a response to the deep trends in world politics that were illuminated by the events of September 11, 2001. [...] This is what the new Bush strategy gets right. What the United States has not yet sorted out is how to go about implementing the new approach. We have done far better on identifying the ends than the means."

N: When I said "illuminated by 9/11" it was the fact that globalization is speeding up, accelerating. The information age was changing the nature of power. That is what was illuminated by 9/11, and that is what Bush got right. Which is that you had to understand these changes. But what he got wrong was thinking that you could do this coercively. And that you could exploit the American model by coercing it to success. And he made a huge mess out of that. What I argue in the book is that if you are interested in exporting democracy, it is better done by soft power than by hard power. If it is soft power, then others have an ability to interpret it, change it, alter it for their own purposes. If it is hard power, they have no choice. With soft power, there is greater room for diversity, with hard power, there is less.

Q: Does this imply that democracy is the best form of government and should thus supersede other forms that still exist?

N: Democracy is very much in the *zeitgeist*. If you look at the number of countries that have become democratic over the last half century, it has been increasing. Right now, it is slipping back a bit. But if you ask me, over the next half century, there will be more than today, not less. Some will disagree and say Russia is an example of a country becoming more autocratic. There is considerable argument about this. I think as you get more economic growth, development of larger middle classes, growing desire for participation, you are more likely to have demands for various types of forms of participation that are often lumped together as 'democracy'. But they won't always look much like the United States.

Q: My last set of questions deal with 'public deliberation'. Would you say that the intellectuals' 'soft power' should counterbalance the government's 'hard power' – its formal institutional design – by providing an informal arena of discussion and debate among the public?

N: Soft power is the ability to attract. And intellectuals express ideas that are compelling, and that can attract both at home and abroad. But I would hope that soft power doesn't have to just counterbalance governmental hard power. I would hope that it would alter it. Intellectuals criticizing torture at Guantánamo don't do this just to attract people overseas that some Americans oppose that. They also want to change the government so that it has more attractive policies at home.

Q: Would you go so far as to call this missionary work?

N: 'Missionary' usually implies that you know the whole truth and that you are preaching it. I would say that there is a commitment to certain values and to certain truths. And that there is an interest in having that understood by other people both at home and abroad. If I think of a missionary, I think of somebody who has the answer, usually a religious answer, which is absolute, and they are going to convert people to it. Maybe this is a question of my own view. I have a feeling that one tries to think one's way through a question and come to an answer which may be more right than wrong, but not always a hundred percent certain. And then try to persuade other people of it. If this is missionary, then yes, but it is a different kind of missionary.

Q: How do you evaluate public deliberation as a feature of present-day democracy? To put it differently: Would a version of democracy lacking public deliberation be of equal value?

N: No, I think there has to be freedom of thought, and freedom of expression. Somebody said that there is a difference between democracy and liberal democracy. Fareed Zakaria calls it 'illiberal democracy'. I don't find great value in illiberal democracy. I think liberal democracy is of much greater value.

Iran has elections, but only candidates that are approved by the mullahs can run. And if you say things which are critical of government you are thrown into jail. That is illiberal democracy. They do have elections, but it is not liberal democracy. In Great Britain or France you can criticize the government and form an opposition party, go on television and say things that the BBC – which is owned by the government – doesn't censor just because you are critical of the government.

Q: Does that mean that intellectuals – guiding public deliberation in the United States – make a qualitative difference when it comes to judging various forms of democracy, such as Iran, Great Britain, or France?

N: Right. I think public criticism is essential to soft power. Something like Abu Ghraib is inexcusable. The fact that Americans have this society in which people can write in a free press that Abu Ghraib is inexcusable – that is a dimension that gives America a better soft power. Even though the government destroys it, there is a civil society to restore it.

Q: Professor Nye, thank you very much for your time.

N: Thank you, and good luck with your study.

Clyde V. Prestowitz, Jr.

Founder and President, Economic Strategy Institute
Washington, D.C.

Q: Mr. Prestowitz, what audience do you have in mind for your publications?

P: As an author, you hope to sell as many books as possible. So you hope the audience is everyone – the more broadly people read it, the better I like it. A book like *Rogue Nation* is ultimately aimed at trying to effect policy changes, so inevitably, you have to have in mind policy makers and the people who influence policy makers: Academics, media commentators, members of Congress, people in the foreign policy web.

But at the same time, I was thinking of the community from which I myself came. I grew out of a very conservative, middle-American, evangelical Christian, patriotic, super-American environment – kind of like the Bush political base. In a way, I had in mind my own family because within my own family, there is a great divide between me and the rest: Half of them are more on my side of the issues, the other half think I am a Communist. In the circles in which I travel at the moment – which are elite, liberal, international circles – there is a bit of a fear, and also a condescension, and maybe even a bit of contempt for those kind of people. They are seen as right-wing crackers, or Christian freaks, or something like that. Now I know those people, and they are basically good people. They have good intentions, they want to do good. The problem is that they don't actually understand what is happening in the world. They have a very skewed understanding of it. But even more importantly, they don't understand what their own government is doing. Whether you accept their theology or not, they are sincerely Christians trying to do good, according to their religious lights. If they really knew what their government was doing in many cases, they would be appalled. And I was trying to show them that. I was trying to say: "Look, folks, I know you have good intentions, I came from you, I understand you, but let me show you how the world really is, and how your government is really acting. Let me show you how the people like Bush that you have championed and elected are really undermining, subverting, acting contrary to the values that you uphold." Take the environment: These people I am talking about are concerned about the environment. They are taught that they should be good preservers of the environment. The whole Bush/Cheney policy has been totally contrary to that.

Q: So there is an 'education project' involved in what you do?

P: Yes, of course. I run a think tank. The whole purpose of a think tank is to educate. In *Rogue Nation*, I was trying to aim at the middle-American conservative base as well as the policy elite, and say: "It is so hard to see yourself as others see you. Let me show you how others are seeing us, and let me show you how we impact on others without realizing it. And if you knew that – because I know you have good intentions – you would try to change what we are doing."

Q: What does your audience expect from you? Concrete policy proposals, or rather a visionary framework of American ideals?

P: In every book, the last chapter is always the what-to-do chapter, so of course you have policy proposals. But the thrust of this book is really to reveal, to let people see a perspective that they have been blind to – and doing that in the certain conviction that if they really saw things as they really are, their own values would force them to change their policies.

Q: You mention values and people's good intentions. How do you evaluate morality in politics? Would you say it is the task of an authority somewhat above the fray of everyday politics to keep an eye on the moral aspects of governing?

P: Of course. It is impossible to divorce moral aspects from policy discussion. Everybody, even the crassest political actor, responds to policy and legislative issues based on some set of beliefs about what is better, and what is worse. And it is almost impossible to divorce that from moral considerations. When writing *Rogue Nation*, I was particularly concerned along those lines.

The Bush era has been particularly bad, but it goes beyond that. I think that US policy has increasingly diverged from what I have always felt were fundamental American values. As we have diverged, we have gotten into more and more trouble. I was trying to make that clear and to get a return to what I think of as a more principled American position.

Q: What is the balance of power like between the world of 'thinkers' – academia, the think tanks – and the world of 'doers' in practical politics?

P: The world of ideas – the academics, the think tankers, the commentators – is clearly the key. There is this famous remark of John Maynard Keynes: He said that even the most hardened, practical business man of affairs who thinks himself totally objective and unaffected by theologies and theories is in fact the slave of some defunct economist. This is true because all the people in positions of power, when they make decisions, they have to make them on the basis of some status, some theory, some rationale for doing what they are doing. Most people don't have time to think of a rationale, and typically they may not even be aware of the rationale they are using. But they inevitably use one. So the people who develop those rationales, and sell them, and imprint them, are ultimately the determiners of our fate.

Q: Why did you choose to found a think tank, a position somewhat apart from practical politics?

P: The reason I founded the think tank is that at a particular moment in time, three things conversed. In the US, most of the top government positions are politically appointed. I found myself in a situation in which it was impossible for me to remain in the government. But I wanted to continue to try to influence the policies that I saw being developed. I couldn't do that in the government, so I had to find a way to do it outside the government. The classic way to do that in the US is to go to a think tank. But I had the problem that most of the think tanks were contrary to my view, so I had to form my own. At that moment, I had some supporters who were willing to put up money, so I was able to form my own think tank. At one point, I did have the opportunity to go into the Clinton administration, but I decided not to do so.

Q: Trying to influence policies – is that what a 'public intellectual' does?

P: Yes, right.

Q: Is it still an appropriate term, i.e. does it still point to something relevant these days?

P: Very much so, yes.

Q: Looking back at history, the American intellectual seems to have lived with a tension from the beginning: On the one hand, a need to keep a critical distance from society, while on the other, a desire to intervene in that same society. What do you make of this, given that the majority of intellectuals today are affiliated with academia, the government, or a think tank?

P: There is some tension. The heart of the question really is the funding: How is a public intellectual funded? Unless you are independently wealthy, as a public intellectual you need to find funding somehow. Typically the places where you find funding are philanthropic organizations, foundations like the Rockefeller Foundation or the Ford Foundation, or wealthy individuals, or corporations, or labor unions – those are the classic places. All of them have their own views, and things that they are trying to promote. What tends to happen is that as a public intellectual you find funding from like-minded people. It could be argued that you are just reflecting their views, you are just bought and paid for, and that is a critique that is often made of think-tank people, and in some cases it is true. But more normally, it is that you find founders who share your views and think that you are a good proponent of those views, and who are willing to support you.

Q: Would you say that the authority of intellectuals has increased since September 11, possibly because of a demand on the side of the American public for someone to explain their nation's foreign policy to them? This would challenge a notion of the intellectuals' gradual decline as proclaimed by the likes of Richard Hofstadter, Zygmunt Bauman, or Richard Posner...

P: I disagree with the idea that there was a decline in the influence of public intellectuals. There is an anti-intellectual tradition in the US, but what is interesting in that regard is that the Right, in this case the conservative Republican base, would probably be described as anti-intellectual by people like Hofstadter and Posner – and in some sense, that is correct. But how did they achieve power? They created think tanks. They created their own television network – Fox News. They became very aggressive in promoting ideas, the *Wall Street Journal* became their arm. In my view, many of these ideas are know-nothing ideas, but they found that in order to gain power they had to have a rationale. And they developed a rationale, and they sold it.

Q: Is it possible to pin this down to a specific date, though? A point in time when the public feels the need for orientation?

P: No, I don't think there is a certain date. The public has always felt that need. I don't see some kind of clear dividing line between 'now the public intellectual is important' and 'now he or she is not'.

Q: Setting the frame a bit wider, a recent period in history – postmodernity – has as its central notion one of basic relativism: The ultimate, universal truth is non-existent. Does this affect public intellectual work in any way, specifically the claim to truth and validity in what you have to say?

P: There is an interesting paradoxical tension here: The rise of modern Liberalism has been accompanied by a rise of relativistic ethical thought. That viewpoint is ultimately in contradiction to what I have been trying to say. But I would argue that modern Liberalism is internally contradictory.

To use a concrete example, Liberalism is a champion of women's rights, at least in the West. In fact, this is kind of a litmus test: If you are not a champion of women's rights, you can't be a Liberal. But that is a value. Karen P. Hughes goes to Saudi Arabia and tells the women that they should be driving and take off their abayas. If you are relativistic, if you really believe in moral relativism, you don't care what happens to the Saudi women, and if one society has one set of values, and we have ours, so well? Why do we care about genocide in Darfur? You might say: They are doing their thing, and we are doing ours. But Liberals are very much concerned about genocide in Darfur. I think Liberals have a problem with their ethical philosophy, and I believe that ultimately they are not relativist. My position is not in contradiction to Liberalism, it is an affirmation of the values we all share.

Q: Is there a general consensus across political affiliations within the US that the American version of democracy should be disseminated throughout the world?

P: There is a widespread view – a belief – in the US that American democracy represents the vanguard of human progress, and that everybody else is evolving and developing in our direction, and that paradise will be when everybody is like us. And that we do have a mission, and a duty to hasten this progress, and to help, enable, or even force others to be more in the mode of American democracy. That is a widespread view on both the Left and the Right.

Q: "The chief reason Americans are blind to their own empire is their implicit belief that every human being is a potential American, and that his or her present national or cultural affiliations are an unfortunate, but reversible accident." Taking into account this quote from the chapter 'The Unacknowledged Empire', how important is it that the United States remains the only superpower?

P: I feel that being the sole superpower, the global hegemon, is corrosive to America. It is harmful. Maintaining our position as the hegemon is not something that we should be striving to do.

There is a well-known European leader, one of the grand old men of Europe, Étienne Davignon, who was the European commissioner for competition and trade, and he articulated this very well when he told me: "In 1948, America was all powerful, you had 15 million men under arms, you were the only one who had the atomic bomb, you were more than 50% of the global GDP, you could have done whatever you wanted to do. The great thing about America at that time was that it sheathed its power. It created multilateral institutions. It committed itself to consultation, and to a kind of international rule of law. Of course, you were the biggest guys on the block, and you usually got your way, but not always, and you agreed to consult. It was a somewhat globally democratic process. The thing that made America so attractive in the post-war period was that America defined its own national interest in terms of the betterment and in terms of the interests of other countries. That was tremendously attractive and powerful: The way you enhanced your power by sheathing it." That is what we ought to do now. We ought to withdraw some. Part of the problem is that in a way other countries are able to be a bit irresponsible. Japan, Korea, and the EU are able to be a bit irresponsible because they are not fully accountable for their own security and international relations. At the same time, we – because of our overwhelming presence and power – are also able to be a bit irresponsible. We would be better off getting back to a position where everybody has to be responsible.

Q: For Europe, that would include stepping up in military terms?

P: Probably, yes. One of the great things about the EU is that it has established a large and growing zone of peace and stability without the use of
military power. Maybe the Europeans have found a better way to do some
of this stuff. A reduction of US power projection around the world would
inevitably resolve in some increase in the military spending and focus of
other countries. I am not advocating that the US should just suddenly
withdraw. Clearly that has to be a process of caution and agreement
among the major players. I expect the US to continue to be in a NATO
alliance, and in alliance with Japan, Korea, and others, but simply to have
a smaller role in the alliance.

*Q: Some thinkers have pointed to a certain European hypocrisy when it
comes to judging America's role in the world – for example, you quote
Robert Kagan in your book. Is there a grain of truth in what he said?*

P: There is a grain of truth in what he said, but only a grain. He misstated
and overstated much of his case. He reflected in his writing what I would
call a typical, classic American condescension to Europe. It is a very
complicated psychology. Kagan and many in those circles have a very
complicated love-hate relationship with Europe. Many of them feel that
Europe is a bit arrogant, and condescending, and elitist toward America,
and they feel the sting of that. The reason they feel the sting is that
somewhere in their consciousness – or subconsciousness – they have that
sense of inferiority to the European elite. So they react to that by over-
compensating and by constantly denigrating Europe and European efforts.
In the US, there is this steady repetition and drumbeat of 'those poor
Europeans' – a kind of *schadenfreude*: "High taxes, high unemployment,
low growth, aging societies, they can't get their act together, we have to
save them from themselves all the time. They just need to become more
like us." This is a very skewed and unrealistic view of Europe, but it is a
common one.

*Q: How do you evaluate public deliberation as a feature of present-day
democracy? Is it possible to imagine a version of democracy without it?*

P: It is hard to imagine democracy without public deliberation, but
clearly there are different forms of democracy around the world, and
some of them have more deliberation than others. I actually think there is
such a thing as too much democracy, there is such a thing as too much
deliberation. And some democracies are more effective than others.

Those that are most effective are not necessarily the ones that have the most deliberation. Obviously, the US is a relatively, reasonably well operating country in comparison to others. But there are serious weaknesses in our democracy. Our democracy is not effectively addressing many of the fundamental issues facing this society.

Q: Are the public intellectuals the ones who might improve the quality of American democracy?

P: They cannot command it, of course. But they can certainly point out and indicate what we need to do and how we need to do it. They can try to create a public base of support for achieving this kind of change – that is the role of a public intellectual.

One of the weaknesses of our democracy which also makes it difficult for a public intellectual to build this support is the way we have structured the electoral districts in the US, and the way that we finance our politics. This has led to a situation which makes it extremely difficult to achieve change. The districts are gerrymandered: If you look at the electoral districts of Iowa, they are all little squares of about the same size. Iowa looks like a grid. Each representative is elected from a territory that is about the same size, with about the same number of people as the next guy. Iowa does its districting based strictly on how many people live in a particular area, without regard to whether those people are Republicans, Democrats, Blacks, Whites, Hispanics, or what have you. But if you look at North Carolina, Mississippi, and a lot of other states, you see very funny shaped districts. Sometimes, one part of the district is not even connected to another part of the district. And you say: Who did *that*? The way they did that was: All the Blacks live in that particular area, and so they put all the Blacks in one district. The Blacks elect one guy, but then they have no influence in other electoral districts. A state legislator determines the size of these districts. And if the state legislator is Republican, they will often try to draw the districts in order to maximize the number of Republicans elected by the state. And if the state legislator is Democrat, they will do the same thing for Democrats. Most of the 435 members of the House of Representatives are thus in what we call 'safe seats', which means that they are elected year after year after year because it is a safe district. They really don't have any contest, except with any challenger who might arise within their party. To beat off these challengers, they need to raise money. So their real constituency is not so much the voters in their district as it is the people who provide them the money. The safe district enhances the power of the money. The US Congress has increasingly become a body that is controlled by particular interests that are not necessarily in the public interest, and that are extremely difficult to change. This is why we are not effectively addressing the major issues in our society. And it is why our democracy is sick. Our democracy is not necessarily the form that I would recommend to other countries.

Q: Mr. Prestowitz, thanks a lot for sharing your thoughts with me.

P: You are very welcome.

Anne-Marie Slaughter

Director of Policy Planning, United States Department of State
Bert G. Kerstetter '66 University Professor of Politics and International Affairs, Princeton University, NJ

Q: I would like to start with a quote from the preface of your book The Idea That Is America: *"We have lost our way in the world. To find it again, we must ask ourselves, and openly debate, a key question: What role should America play in the world?" Who is "we"? In other words: What audience do you have in mind for your publications?*

S: The "we" there was aimed at the broadest possible audience. I deliberately wrote my book for an audience that reads *USA Today,* or the *Reader's Digest,* and indeed I have got a piece that should come out in *Reader's Digest.* I wrote it for people who would read books recommended by Oprah Winfrey, on the theory that this debate, the debate about what our values are, and how we stand for them, cannot be just an elite debate. And in part that is because the premise of my book is that in the end the American public insists on a values-based foreign policy. Efforts to turn purely to interest always generate their own backlash. As an American, I believe we have to have a values-based foreign policy, but I think we need a very broad debate on what those values are and what it means to stand for them. And that debate has been captured by a very small part of the political spectrum.

Q: Is there an aspect of 'public schooling', or an educational project behind what you do?

S: I think so. I am no historian, and there are many great texts on American history. But I definitely felt that in part with the decline of civics education which many people have lamented – from William Bennett on the Left to the ABA, the American Bar Association, on the Right and the National Urban Institute – that it was time to tell stories from our founding to the Civil War to the New Deal to the Civil Rights Movement that emphasized the combination of great patriotism and active willingness to criticize the government and the country when it strays from its values – or betrays its values. So yes, part of writing for such a broad audience was exactly a book that I hoped could be used in high school and college history courses.

Q: Why did you choose American foreign policy as one of the areas to focus on in your book?

S: Why couple history with foreign policy? Partly because that is what I do. And I was persuaded that there is no reason to read Anne-Marie Slaughter on American history. There is some reason to read Anne-Marie Slaughter on American foreign policy because that is what I do.

The reason I was interested in writing about American history was precisely because I think how we understand our past – 'we' meaning the American people – and how we understand our values is critical to what I think of as finding our way again in the world. So the aim of the book was twofold: To recover an account of who we are that was consistent with being sharply critical when necessary, and to define patriotism in the way that Carl Schurz does: "My country, right or wrong; if right, to be kept right; and if wrong, to be set right." And then to use that concept to say: "Ok, if that is how we understand ourselves, here is what we need to do in the world. Here is what a values-based foreign policy that is genuinely consistent with our values would look like."

Q: How would you define the term 'public intellectual'? And is the term still relevant in public discourse?

S: Yes. Very much so. There is a very clear and important role for public intellectuals. It is a concept that is well understood in academia. You can be an absolute top scholar at a top school and not be a public intellectual. There is a clear route to becoming a public intellectual. You have to start writing for a broader public, and that generally starts with newspaper op-eds, pieces in policy journals and journals of broader public interest than purely academic journals – such as *Foreign Affairs*, or *Foreign Policy*, or *The American Prospect*, or *The National Interest*. Which means you have to write differently. You have to learn how to communicate with that broader audience. It means giving speeches, and writing trade books rather than academic books. Generally when you do so, you may well lose a certain amount of the respect on the part of your purely academic colleagues. They will recognize what you are doing and may value it for what it is, but what is most valued at universities is still scholarly work, which is as it should be. As a dean, I still value pure academic work the most highly because it is pushing out the frontiers of knowledge, which is the comparative advantage of research universities. But I also think that there is a very important role for those intellectuals who can do it to turn not only to broader public education, but also the stirring of public debate.

Q: American intellectuals seem to have faced a difficult situation from the beginning. On the one hand, there was the need to keep a distance from society, yet on the other, there was a desire to intervene in that same society. What do you make of this tension? What about the intellectuals' claim to act autonomously, given that the majority of them are employed by the government, by universities, or by one of the big think tanks these days?

S: I don't think of it as a tension that cannot be resolved. There are multiple ways to negotiate this tension.

The first – the easy one – is the distinction between think tank intellectuals and academic intellectuals. The person who finishes their Ph.D. and heads to Brookings – versus the person who finishes their Ph.D. and takes an academic position – is choosing from the very outset to be both a research scholar and a public intellectual. Because this is exactly the role that think tanks play. That role has increased. When I was in college, between twenty-five and thirty years ago, there were many more top faculty members, people like Stanley Hoffmann at Harvard, who played equally in the academic and the policy world. But in the intervening thirty years, academia has become much more specialized, and much more methodologically opaque. And similarly, there are many more think tanks. So what was once a kind of natural bridge for certain individuals, what was once a world in which you could have one foot in the policy world, and one foot in pure academia, has now in most cases become two specialized occupations.

Q: It seems the situation for American intellectuals has not become significantly easier. A distinctive feature of 'postmodernity' is a notion of relativism: the assumption that a universal truth is basically non-existent. How do you reconcile this notion with the claim to truth and validity you make in your most recent book, for instance?

S: I am a pretty un-reconstructed modernist. I am not a postmodernist. I accept some of the insights of postmodernism. I am certainly alert to the nuances of cultural perspectives. As I write in the book, I grew up moving between two cultures, and now I am in China for a year, so I am no stranger to cultural differences, different intellectual perspectives. But I do not believe that there is no truth, or that everything is relative. What I believe is that there is no absolute truth, that the nature of truth is perpetual contestation – but within what I call 'a zone of legitimate difference'. We may not be able to say what is *the* truth, but we can say what is a falsehood. At some point there is a line, and it is always a difficult line to draw. Lawyers spend their life trying to draw difficult lines. But there is a line between saying "there are multiple versions of the good life," and saying "to be tortured is wrong." The notion that from some perspectives, for instance, to be deprived of basic sustenance, or to be subject to intense physical or mental pain – it is not okay, no matter what your culture is.

I have spent a lot of my academic career engaged in debates with postmodernists, and I don't know what the term for *me* is – maybe you could call it 'Enlightened Modernist'. That is definitely where I am. I got ridiculed in my early academic career for believing in liberal progress narratives, but I still do. And as I say in my book, you can't grow up in Virginia as a woman in the 1960s, and look around the United States today, and not believe in progress. When I was growing up, African-Americans were still completely segregated; racism was rampant. And the idea that you would have a woman Secretary of State, a black woman Secretary of State, a primary for the Democratic presidential nominee run between an African-American and a woman – you might as well have been living on the moon.

Q: Taking another step toward the present, what about the time period from 2001 until today? Would you say that intellectuals have regained some authority, possibly due to the public's demand for orientation regarding questions like, what is America's position in the world since 9/11? If so, do you believe the view of the intellectual as being in decline held by writers such as Richard Hofstadter, Zygmunt Bauman, Richard Posner, and others, would have to be challenged?

S: I certainly don't see a decline. It is right that in the wake of a major trauma there is a tremendous demand for narratives and concepts that allow people to make sense of what is a deeply frightening and suddenly disorienting world. That is why I titled my book 'Keeping Faith with Our Values in a Dangerous World'. It was an effort to reach people who felt it was a dangerous world – whether or not I do.

What has been true is that it has advantaged public intellectuals on the Right much more than the Left. The reason is embedded in what Barack Obama has gotten in trouble for: The Right responded to 9/11 in much more traditional, patriotic terms. The immediate wearing of a flag pin on the lapel. The American flag everywhere. I found that response somewhat misplaced because people from over eighty countries died in the attacks. It was an attack on not just America, but on a set of global values – and yet the majority of Americans responded in traditional patriotic terms. And that meant that Conservatives who framed 9/11 as solely an attack on the United States had much more public purchase than many public intellectuals on the Left. Many prominent left-wing commentators, such as Richard Falk and Christopher Hitchens, dramatically shifted their traditional positions and supported the war in Afghanistan. But they were deeply uncomfortable with the traditional iconography of patriotism. And that left them a little high and dry.

That is one of the reasons I wanted to write my book: A perception that, particularly in times of crisis, there have to be ways to appeal to patriotism, and to do it sincerely, not falsely, in a far broader and more capacious way. So I don't think there has been a decline, I think there has been a shift in who took over the leading of public debate. The traditional Left didn't know how to take on the issues of the day in a way that was compelling to the public of the day.

Q: Do you feel that the 'public of the day' expects you to come forward with concrete policy proposals, or rather with a visionary framework of American ideals? In your introduction, you argue that "America is a place, a country, a people, but also an idea." And a couple of pages later on, you say: "[T]his book is about far more than words (...). We must translate our ideals into concrete plans and policies."

S: I think it is both. To some extent, this goes back to 'are you purely in the policy world?' Because if you are purely in the policy world, you will only have impact if you are very specific. The people who really shape what the government is going to do next are people who have very concrete ideas and who follow all the twists and turns of the policy process, whether it is in the White House, or in Congress. But the people who have the greatest impact on the public are people who can reach for broader concepts. I would use Fareed Zakaria's book *The Future of Freedom* as an example: a concept of an 'illiberal democracy'. That book is bigger on concepts than it is on policy proposals. But you are only going to have that kind of weight with the public if you are also validated as an expert. And the only way to be validated as an expert is to have more than just grand ideas. You don't have to be as specific as the think tank crowd, but you can't just get out and write about grand visions without demonstrating that you know what you are talking about and that you have real expertise in an area so that you can convert the concepts to specific proposals. They won't be as specific as the kind of proposal that gets passed in the next round of legislation, but they have to be at least at the level of specificity to go into a state-of-the-union speech.

Q: To stick with the idea of 'the grand vision' you mentioned – do you think it might be necessary after 9/11 to create a new, uniting concept or even a myth for America, beyond all political trench warfare? Or will the very existence of adversarial political camps start a controversial debate that is good for the nation? In your chapter on tolerance, you argue that there was a "spirit of unity" in the immediate aftermath of the attacks. But then you say that "the spirit of unity proved all too short-lived. The years following the September 11 attacks have been some of the most partisan in memory, embittered by opposing views..."

S: Well, I do think we need to pull more together. But I don't think that means we need one line. I am an American lawyer, and the American legal process believes in the adversary process as a form of positive conflict. It is bounded conflict, it is not anything goes. But it does recognize real value in contestation. I don't want a country where everybody pulls in the same direction, and everyone has the same narrative. That would be worrisome. We need a kind of debate, though, and a kind of frame for that debate that accepts the good faith of different positions.

What I think has happened – it has happened often in American political life, but it is very damaging right now – is a kind of debate that is much more ad hominem than focused on the actual issues, and presumes that if you disagree, it is because you are a bad person, rather than because you have a different means of getting to common ends. So I am calling for agreement on a set of common ends very broadly. An agreement on the value of debate, and of tolerance of different viewpoints. That is quite critical. This allows us to have very robust contestation of important issues, but in a way that will actually move us forward rather than divide us on a very personal and intolerant level.

Q: Who should provide the framework for this debate you are talking about?

S: Within the United States, I have actually been quite pleased with this political campaign. To date, it has been a genuinely democratic debate with multiple perspectives. The ability to sustain a campaign where you have many more voters engaged than usual, where you have the blogosphere, you have lots of actual debates, that is what we have needed, and I have been very pleased with the results. More broadly, I think we need a conversation among democracies that runs far beyond the United States. What the US needs is to hear from many other countries, and recognize that they are speaking from positions of difference, but it is legitimate difference. We do not have to agree, but we do have to listen and we have to acknowledge alternate validity.

Q: Talking about America's relationship with the rest of the world, the issue of US leadership comes to mind. Would you agree that there is a general consensus among American intellectuals, eclipsing political affiliations to a certain degree, that the American version of democracy should be disseminated throughout the world? And that if there is any controversy, it is mainly about the most effective way to proceed with this dissemination?

S: I don't agree. I actually think there is increasing consensus that America should be supporting democracy rather than promoting it, across the political spectrum. When I chaired the State Department's Advisory Committee on Democracy Promotion, the one thing everyone agreed on – right and left – was that it should not be promotion, it should be support. That idea actually says there are many different forms of democracy. Different national groups must ground their desire for self-government in their own history and culture. We can support them, and we should support them, but we shouldn't dictate what they do and how they do it. Efforts to do that and to take American democracy as the template for what democracy should look like typically fail.

I think many Americans – at least Americans who are interested in these subjects – have become increasingly aware of what an idiosyncratic form of democracy we have. We are a presidential system, not a parliamentary one. We are an extreme individualist system. On things like freedom of speech, we are so far out on one end of the spectrum of protection that to think that people are going to imitate our system is highly unlikely. Actually the EU has had a big impact there, too. Increasingly, many countries look to EU forms of democracy, not just parliamentary versus presidential, but also civil legal systems, how you draft certain laws...It is an easier model for many countries to adopt.

Q: Another quote from your book seems to fit in here: "Finally, our shared values are essential because they link America to the world. The belief that American values are universal values (...) connects us to other nations." What exactly does "connect" mean?

S: This is exactly where I tried to get back to what our founders understood. There is a Platonic ideal of all these values: liberty, justice, democracy, tolerance, equality... All nations whose people and government are set up in the service of this ideal are connected by it – seeing the shadow on the wall of the cave. But in reality, each nation achieves quite often a quite different version of that ideal. Those differences can be superficial, and they can be quite substantive. Superficially, you can have different rules governing freedom of speech. Substantively, you can say that those differences reflect different notions of social solidarity, e.g. whether it is acceptable to allow hate speech. Or on equality, the differences between the United States and Europe are quite profound in terms of the degree of which it is acceptable to allow the bottom rungs of your society to be really left on their own. Europe has a very different view of that, and yet, as I write in my definition of equality, both systems can be equally committed to an idea of equality because equality is a very complicated idea. You can have really legitimate arguments about what is the best way to try to achieve that ideal, knowing that the ideal is impossible. It is always going to be imperfect. So the connection is the connection of different societies striving in their way to realize these ideals, to reflect these values. That is the connection, but that implies acceptance of difference.

Q: How important is it that the United States remains the sole superpower in the world? You seem to grapple with the issue in your book, for instance in the chapter on liberty, when you say: "The world needs an international order that is similarly adapted to the needs of the twenty-first century. The United States should lead the way and rally other nations to reform the current international order." In the chapter on humility, you argue that "most generally, we must understand our own limits in addressing all the world's problems." How do you like the superpower claim?

S: I don't like the superpower claim. I don't think we are the only super-power now. I think we are the only military superpower, but we are not the only economic superpower. The EU is an equal economic super-power. I don't think we are the only political superpower. We are al-ready in a multipolar world economically and increasingly politically. In a military sense, yes, we are still the world's only superpower, but I don't think military power is all that useful for tackling many of the problems we have to tackle. It is not a power that is relevant in many cases.

I have argued and written that the US must lead on some issues, but not on all issues. Even our style of leadership must be adapted to the rec-ognition that we are in a multipolar world in many dimensions. And that doesn't mean a return to geopolitical competition. It is not that kind of multipolar world. Our military power does mean that no other nation is going to attack us, and we don't need to worry that we can't defend our-selves, although of course with terrorist attacks, military power is not all that helpful. What I argue for is a concept of being *a* leading nation rather than being *the* leading nation on all issues. We need to recognize that there is going to be a whole set of issues on which we need partners, and that part of having partners is letting them take the lead some of the time.

Q: "In foreign policy today, we must again embrace our values as a fighting faith [by] demonstrating why our faith is justified, how in fact a liberal democracy can deliver on its promises for all citizens better than any other form of government can." This seems to imply that the version of democracy America has found for itself could be of significant value for others as well...

S: Yes, that I do believe. This is not American thinking, this is Enlight-enment thinking. It is European originally, and I do believe that these values are universal values, in various versions, adapted to various cul-tures – but not infinitely adapted.

The Soviet Union was not a liberal democracy, and it did not stand for these values in practice. It may have in theory. I believe that these values do hold the best prospects of human flourishing in every country in the world. But a) countries have to find their own way. They can be sup-ported, but you can't impose it. And b) you do have to demonstrate that it works both in your own country and in the way you support other coun-tries. So if you are providing aid to a country that says it stands for the values of equality and liberty, but in fact that government is siphoning off the aid, or not delivering to its people, you are not actually supporting those values. It may well be that, say in Turkey, a religious party that may seem to be quite contrary to these values, is actually delivering to its people a degree of education, and health care, and social space to allow for human flourishing, and allows actual choosing of government. You have to look at that and ask yourself on the real measure of these values – rather than the rhetorical measure – who is actually living up to them.

Q: I would like to move on to the issue of morality in politics. How would you evaluate the discussion of morality in politics? Would you say it is the task of an authority who is somewhat above the shoals of everyday politics to keep an eye on the moral aspects of governing?

S: I don't believe in legislating public morality. In that sense, I am a liberal humanist in that I certainly believe strongly in freedom of conscience, freedom of expression. That means that people can choose what to believe or what not to believe. My husband is an atheist, and we talk openly about the vital importance, particularly in American politics, of not discriminating against atheists anymore than discriminating against believers. That also means that morality is personal as long as it doesn't hurt others. You can't murder. But you can look at pornography – as long as it is not child pornography – all you want.

I don't believe in the public legislation of morality other than to the extent of preventing immorality from actively doing harm to others. On the other hand, there is – at least in the United States – a vital civic culture that is very essential to making the political system work and giving meaning to national identity. Are those moral values? They can be described as moral values, but they can equally be described as civic values. It may be true that in the United States that line is a very blurry one, but I think it is very much the business of anyone engaged in public life to take our commitments to those values – which are enshrined in our Constitution – seriously, and to debate them, and to make them a part of citizens' public discussions and commitments to individual candidates and the public issues.

Q: I would like to quote another passage from the chapter on faith: "We need first to recover our faith as a people in our ability to live up to and implement our values [which requires] a frank look at our failings, an open acknowledgment that in many ways our society has lost its way. We must be able to diagnose our ills..." Should there be a certain group of people – possibly the public intellectuals – whose lead the public would be able to follow?

S: Yes, as long as it is clear that that group need not be an elite.

One of the great things about blog culture is that anyone can participate who has the knowledge, the time, and the determination to commit to that kind of public debate. 21st-century public intellectuals are people who are willing to engage in that debate, and seriously, not just to issue polemics, but to actively engage. To devote time, to devote energy, to devote whatever resources they may have, to direct life decisions in that direction of wanting to shape public opinion and commit to advancing a larger public project.

This is the project our founders envisaged. When you look back to the 18th century, there is of course plenty of romanticism – I grew up in the hometown of Thomas Jefferson, and I know his virtues and his flaws – but they were a group of people who undertook a great public project, and who believed fervently in it, and believed in its value for the United States and globally. For the sake of the United States, and for the sake of all the countries the United States influences whether it wants to or not, there is still a very important role for that public class. The difference today is that although there are traditional ways of becoming a public intellectual, there are also individuals whom I communicate with now on a fairly regular basis through blogs, who are not your traditional public intellectuals, but who have found a way to play a role.

Q: "The tone of those debates is often fierce and divisive, but the disagreement and dissent that fuel them is an essential part of American life (...). We must also expand national debates beyond the politicians and pundits (including me!). These debates must genuinely engage the American people." Taking up this quote from your conclusion, my last question is: How would you evaluate the importance of public deliberation as a feature of present-day democracy?

S: I certainly think that you can have democracies in which public deliberation is much less vital than in the United States because it is less necessary in countries that are much more ethnically, or religiously, or culturally homogeneous. Living here in China, when I talk to people about the role of law in the United States, they often say to me, "we don't like having things written down, and made transparent and public and debated because we think they are more real if they are felt rather than objectified." I understand that argument, and I see it also in various European countries. But in a country as diverse as the United States, just hugely diverse, and becoming more so constantly – in the twenty years that I have been in teaching, my classroom has changed dramatically in color and in ethnicity –, in that kind of a country, these things have to be public, and they have to be debated. What may be implicit for me is not implicit for the Mexican immigrant who has just arrived, the Chinese-American, the recent immigrant from a former Soviet country.

A lot of my emphasis on the public value of active contestation is where I started: America is a people, and a country, and a place, but it is also an idea. It is that idea which is an abstract idea, and which is constantly being filled and refilled with different concrete expressions – that is what holds us together. In that sense, the view that I put forward is more relevant for American democracy than it would be for many other countries.

Q: Is this what American intellectuals are supposed to do: Fill the idea?

S: That is a good point. I think the best example I could give is: Take public intellectuals in France versus in the United States.

In France, you can be a public intellectual by being a *philosophe*: A philosopher, or a literary critic, or a cultural critic. People read you, people debate you. Your debates about the contemporary nature of French society can take place in a context of a review of Racine or Molière or a contemporary French author. That is not going to happen in the United States. Yes, we have our own culture, but we don't have a common enough artistic culture, or philosophic traditions, or even religious traditions to allow intellectuals to be specialists in those areas and still reach a mass audience. So our broad platform for debate is indeed the nature of our public, the nature of our public discourse, the nature of our politics, the nature of our identity, the nature of our values.

Q: So there is a specific type of American intellectual?

S: There is a specific type of American *public* intellectual. There are American intellectuals in all those areas I just mentioned, as there are in any other country. And certainly we have a grand university tradition borrowed from the European university tradition. I don't want to say that there is a different kind of American intellectual, but I think the public intellectuals in the United States are much more likely to be politically activist.

Q: Professor Slaughter, thank you very much for your time.

S: You are welcome. I enjoyed the conversation.

Nancy Soderberg

Distinguished Visiting Scholar, University of North Florida, FL
Foreign Policy Adviser to the Mayor of New York City,
Michael Bloomberg
Former U.S. Ambassador to the United Nations
Former 3rd ranking official, National Security Council

Q: Ms. Soderberg, what audience do you have in mind for your publications?

S: As an author, you always hope that a million people read your book, but when I wrote this book – *The Superpower Myth* –, it would be students who were trying to figure out their views of the world and America's role in it. The generally informed public – certainly beyond just the think-tank views.

I use the book teaching in my classes, and I tried to write it in such a way that it would give people a sense that there are real people in government, making difficult decisions. They don't always get it right, and they don't always have a crystal ball to see how things are going to move forward. I was trying to explain how the policy process actually, really works. What the book does is exactly that. This is the process side of it. And on the policy side: How naïve it was for the Bush administration to think it was all powerful. The 'Superpower Myth' means: We are unquestionably the most powerful country on earth. We are omnificent and can do whatever we want. We can solve our problems on our own. But the nature of threats shifted. We can only address them as we have international support to do so. So the bottom line is that we need to be the great persuader, and not just the great enforcer. I think the pendulum has swung back a little bit in the last year of the Bush administration when it began to realize that it simply cannot sustain its policy, and that the damage to American interests around the world is significant. The ideologues started to leave the government, too – which helps a lot. The foreign policy establishment changed, the Boltons, the Wolfowitzes, and Rumsfelds have moved out. Condoleezza Rice interestingly has nothing but career people in the State Department now. Cheney is still in the White House, but that's about it.

Q: Is there an 'education project' involved in what you do? Do you intend to provide the American people with a background of knowledge that makes it possible for them to participate effectively in democracy?

S: Not really. I think the American public is actually pretty good at handling democracy. I am not an education expert. It helps to educate students around the world to get more power to them, but that wasn't exactly where I was headed with this book.

Q: The thought came up while reading the introduction: "This book aims to be a testament to the importance of getting right America's leadership role and responsibility in the world. While September 11 demonstrated America's vulnerability, it may also galvanize the public to support a deeper engagement with the rest of the world."

S: I actually think that is happening. Not so much because of the book. I like to think that the book helps shape the debate, but a debate like this tends to be at a fairly elite level. When you have an administration that gets so off course, the American public knows something is wrong. They don't know exactly how to fix it, but they expect America's government to do its job: To protect America and make things work. But they just know something is not right, and this book offers them policy prescriptions. You are not going to get the uneducated eighth grader to read this. But I think it helps putting things into context as a university level book. Students look at it as "ok, now I see what's wrong, and how to fix it, and why it matters," which is a useful way of having things evolve. But mass education – it's not like it sold a million copies. Hopefully, one day it will!

Q: As someone who has worked both in the government and the academy, what does your audience expect from you: concrete policy proposals, or rather a visionary framework of American ideals?

S: This is probably why I wrote this second book – *The Prosperity Agenda*: You want to stay part of the debate, continue to build on your experiences and ideas of how to move forward. The idea of a book like this is really that you need to have America become the force for change on the international stage so that the world sees that America is working on their behalf and in their interest. That means getting on the front end of the developing world's challenges: death, disease, poverty. If America is seen to be doing that, they will be more willing to help us with our challenges which are primarily terrorism and weapons-of-mass-destruction proliferation issues. Right now, the world doesn't trust America. If you look at any of the polls, they are quite devastating on anti-Americanism: Lack of trust, they think we are a military threat. Seven out of eight Muslim countries think we are a military threat to them. So you look at having America shift its course to be seen to be moving on those issues in exchange for them helping us on ours. To a certain extent, the United States has already moved slightly in that direction. It is not talking so much in bravado terms anymore. The Bush administration is not going to move on Kyoto, or the ICC, and some of the other issues. But it has moved quite a bit on HIV/AIDS and poverty in the African Initiative.

Q: Another issue, the worldwide promotion of democracy of the American kind, seems to find broad support, even across the various political camps. Do you agree?

S: I don't think America can go out to the world and promote democracy per se. What we can do is help provide benefits to people that give them the choice. In order to have that you have to have a decent standard of living, a decent education, checks and balances within a society. And when you don't have these, the United States needs to stand up and push back – for instance with what's going on in Russia. We haven't really been too active over the last five years in resisting the move away from democracy. All throughout Latin America, there are major problems, and we have been AWOL on those debates. We can't impose democracy around the world. It has to be from the grassroots up. But the United States can help create the conditions so that democracy can establish itself. Even in Iraq – we invaded the country, and we said we were going to sell this democracy there – we are not really talking about democracy unless we can get security and stability. Democracy is not the sort of thing you can go around with and export, but you can help support it and make it flourish.

Q: How important is it that the United States remains the only superpower in the world?

S: That is the wrong question. It is not a question of "are we sitting here, trying to be the most powerful country on earth?" What we are trying to do is continue to grow and prosper, and we are so far ahead of everybody else that there is no one on the horizon. The economic leadership over the last seven years has damaged our position – the falling dollar is the best indicator of others losing confidence in America. Our military is a wreck. We have problems on a number of levels. But we are still the biggest power around. As you combine all the other countries' militaries together, they are still not even close to where we are. And I don't see anyone challenging that in the near future. We are going to be the only superpower, we don't even have to really try. It is what it is. The question is how to use that power. Is there a way to use it to further and strengthen America? I believe there is. We have to be the great persuader, and not the enforcer. Instead of being an anchor on these issues, we have to be a magnet out there pushing the world in the right direction, and we just have not been in the last seven years.

Q: Is this what you mean when you state in the chapter 'Force and Diplomacy' that "Clinton understood the need for the United States to lead the world as the first non-imperialist superpower" ...?

S: The world is hungry for the right American leadership. It is like children resisting rules, regulations, and boundaries, but they also want them. They want leadership. That is a little bit too paternalistic a way to put it, but when you have the biggest, most powerful superpower in the world making the wrong mistakes, everybody suffers.

When we invade Iraq and get it all wrong, when we lose the ball on Afghanistan, when we pull Iran so that they are just moving forward on nuclear weapons, not focusing on democracy, when we trigger anti-Americanism so that people are not working with us on the challenges that we face, when we make one mistake after the other, we are feeding into the narratives of the terrorists in a way that is creating more terrorists, not less. It is just not smart.

The rest of the world wants us to be out there, fighting AIDS, death, disease, poverty, trying to negotiate the Israeli-Palestinian crisis, the Kashmir crisis because only the United States can do that. If we don't lead, the rest of the world is like cats and dogs arguing about it. But once America says "here is where we are going to come out," and if we largely get it right, the rest of the world will follow.

Q: How should the United States go about conveying this claim to leadership?

S: Doing it. They have to do it. They have to work with the other countries, negotiate. It is much easier to go out on your own and just do what you want to do, but the results aren't as good. So it is getting in there, strengthening the non-proliferation treaty, working on the disarmament, not invading North Korea and Iran, but negotiating with our allies, keeping the nuclear genie in the box, doing something on the Arab-Israeli peace process, getting ahead of the curve on the environmental crisis, working with the international community.

Bush has actually done some of this. He has done quite a bit on debt reduction, but he gets no credit because the other mistakes still overshadow what he has done. We need to recognize that the United States cannot go it alone on these issues. We need the international community to help keep us faith now. That is annoying, and it is frustrating, but it is the way it is. That is the real world. The experiment of the hegemons in the Bush administration has demonstrated just how dangerous it is when you are trying to fight that reality. It doesn't work.

Q: To quote from the chapter 'Lessons for the President': "Around the world, America's image is declining just when we need strong moral leadership to galvanize world coalitions." How would you evaluate the role of morality in politics? Is it the task of an authority outside the realm of practical politics to prevent us from losing sight of these moral aspects?

S: 'Moral' can be quite a buzzword for some people. It can have countless connotations. In this context, I mean decisions that are true to American values, which is standing up for the rule of law, standing up for the rights of the individual, and making decisions that are really promoting American values – which we have not been doing. So 'moral' leadership not in the religious sense, but in the sense of making better decisions that don't involve torture, and wire-tapping, and locking up suspects and throwing away the key. This is both immoral and not in our interest. It doesn't advance our interests, in fact it is quite damaging to them.

Q: What is the balance of power between the world of thinkers – academia and the think tanks – and the world of practical politics?

S: Academics have very little power. Every academic who wants to write on public policy needs to have worked in an administration to get a sense of just how difficult decisions are. That said, academics can help shape and inform the debate, and challenge the policies. Journalists are very much in that category as well. Academics play a valuable part in trying to shape the American opinion on how to address issues, and in challenging the facts that an administration puts out by giving different views. The people who are in the government are the ones who actually make the decisions to a degree or two away from the power curb. But academics can be extremely influential as part of that whole checks-and-balances system. It is useful for government officials to go into think tanks and think about what they have been doing, too. Both professions have certain strengths and weaknesses. You never have time to think in government, but you have lots of power. You have lots of time to think, but no power in a think tank. So you need to alternate back and forth a little bit.

Q: American intellectuals obviously alternate in yet another way. From the beginning, they seem to have lived with a certain tension: While trying to keep their distance from society, they also want to intervene in that society. What do you make of this tension, given that today, the majority of intellectuals are employed by the government, universities, or think tanks?

S: There are two factors here. America is a lot more democratic than Europe in a non-elitist way. Europe is still very class-conscious, and stratified, and segregated in terms of the melting pot. We just don't have that issue here. America is more democratic on a fundamental level, in terms of 'anybody can make it here'.

The other factor is 9/11. It woke the country up, people started thinking about these things. People are nervous. The war in Iraq makes people nervous. They don't understand why the price of gas is four dollars. Their own prosperity here is increasingly at risk. They want to know what is really going on here. There is a market for people who can simply explain what is going on. But this also opens it up for demagogues like Lou Dobbs who has single-handedly created the impression that we have an immigration crisis in our country when in fact we don't. We don't let enough immigrants in to do jobs that Americans don't want. They are not terrorists, and they are not undermining our society. They are performing a valuable service. They wouldn't want to be here if people didn't want to hire them. There is a cause from people who are scared, and there is some wrong information, and the wrong people can fill that void.

Q: So 9/11 really is a watershed moment? Has the authority of public intellectuals increased since then due to the public's need for explanations?

S: 9/11 got people more interested in some of these issues. And the war in Iraq has definitely increased the public's interest in these issues. I notice this from my own public speaking: I get a lot more really intense questions on what this all means.

Q: How would you define the term 'public intellectual' and is it still a relevant concept today?

S: Sure, absolutely. I would define it as the elite writers. Most of the commentators on TV would not be considered intellectuals. There is a vibrant intellectual community in the United States that is thriving and flourishing. It is a little scrappier, and a little more plebeian than that in Europe, but equally sophisticated, and equally important in shaping the public's view of America's role in the world.

Q: Is that their main function: To shape the public's view of their nation in the world?

S: No, their main function is to satisfy human quests for knowledge and the purpose of our existence on this earth. Human beings have a vast desire to understand our world. Public policy is a tiny piece of that. It happens to be my piece as I am interested in it, but I think there is a much broader role for intellectuals to play in shaping our understanding and role in life. They keep our life interesting. And this has been going on since probably well before Socrates, he was just the first one that wrote it down.

Q: Ms. Soderberg, thank you very much for your time.

S: You are very welcome.

Strobe Talbott

Former Deputy Secretary of State
President, The Brookings Institution
Washington, D.C.

Q: Mr. Talbott, what audience do you have in mind for your publications?

T: For *The Age of Terror*, Nyan Chanda – my coeditor – and I had in mind as broad an audience as we could get. We just felt that the magnitude of the event, the consequentiality of the event, the degree of public interest in it justified us trying on very short notice to get something out there into the stores that people would find useful in trying to make sense of this horrible development. That is what we tried to do, and I hope we succeeded.

Q: Is there an 'education project' involved in what you do?

T: Yes, I would say that. In fact in my current capacity at the Brookings Institution, we see public education as absolutely vital to what we do.

Q: Why do you choose to focus upon American foreign policies?

T: First of all, Brookings does not exclusively concentrate on foreign policy – far from it. Brookings covers the very wide waterfront that includes domestic issues, international issues, and subjects that subsume both. Foreign policy just happens to be my own career background.

Q: So the focus of your book The Age of Terror *is simply due to the horrendous events? Or is foreign policy in general the number one topic every American citizen should know about?*

T: I would say, given the choice between the two – domestic policy and foreign policy – it is more of the latter. But homeland security is a domestic priority for the U.S. in an increasingly interdependent and sometimes dangerous world.

Q: How would you define the term 'public intellectual'? Do you still deem it appropriate today?

T: I'm not crazy about that term. I know it's out there, there is nothing anyone can do to take it out of circulation. It just doesn't happen to be a term that resonates particularly with me. It sounds doubly exclusive in a way that doesn't make a whole lot of sense. It's exclusive in that it suggests that there are intellectuals and non-intellectuals. I don't think there's a neat dividing line between the two. Second, it distinguishes between public intellectuals and non-public intellectuals, and I don't know what *that* means. That's why it's just not part of my vocabulary.

Q: Leading American thinkers seem to have had an increase in authority with the public since September 11, possibly because people need a guiding voice of reason that can explain the nation's course – would you agree?

T: Yes, intuitively, that sounds correct – and for just the reason that you say. There was a certain market for – and now you have tricked me into using the term – "public intellectuals" back during the Cold War because people needed help in sorting out what was at stake, and what the dangers were, and so on. We haven't had that kind of thing since 9/11 came along.

Q: What does your audience expect from you: concrete policy proposals, or rather a visionary framework of American ideals?

T: I think it behooves those of us who think about these things, and either write or edit books on them, not only to identify problems and ruminate on their nature, but also to come up with concrete policy suggestions. That's very much what we do at Brookings.

Q: American intellectuals seem to have lived with a certain tension from the beginning. On the one hand, there was a need to remain distanced from society, while on the other hand, a desire to intervene in that society. What do you make of the intellectuals' claim to act outside of purpose-driven constraints, given that, these days, most of them are employed by the government, the universities, or a think tank?

T: This is one reason why I don't like the phrase 'public intellectual'. Let's take a couple of examples from ancient history, as it were: Was George F. Kennan a public intellectual when he was ambassador to Moscow, or when he was in Washington as the Founding Director of the Policy Planning Staff of the State Department, and when he was universally known as Mr. X and the father of the containment doctrine? I would say: yes. He happened to be a public intellectual who was on the government payroll. You can't get more public than that, right?

Was Henry Kissinger a public intellectual when he was Secretary of State, using phrases like 'conceptual breakthrough'? He was a government servant, he was an appointed official of the United States government, but he was also a public intellectual.

Is Paul Kennedy a public intellectual, or John Lewis Gaddis? These are outstanding academic historians who have spent literally their whole careers in the academy, and have only indirect or episodic contact with the policy community. Yet the answer is absolutely yes.

I wouldn't say there is tension so much as there is difference in perspective. One thing that made Kennan effective, influential, and revered was that even when he was in a government job, he was able to maintain not only a very high standard of quality of mind and quality of analysis; he was also able to maintain some perspective, and didn't just spout the government line, or summarize the bureaucracy's position on something. Rather he thought and spoke out and wrote independently – which is what I would regard as a good working definition of an intellectual, never mind whether that word is preceded by "public."

Q: What is the balance of power like between the world of thinkers – the think tanks, the universities – and the world of practical politics?

T: It depends on how you define and measure power. It is not even close in terms of who has real power – that is, the power to send troops halfway around the world, to occupy countries, or to put billions of dollars into ventures here, there, or elsewhere like bailing out distressed economies. You have to be in a government position to do that. There is no question about it. You might add the media to your list, by the way. They are also influential, but in a different way. All of these categories overlap. That said, people who are in government are also constrained. They, as individuals, have as much power as the government they work for is willing to allow them to exercise, which is usually pretty incremental – it only becomes truly powerful if the whole government is behind a policy. Even when you are talking about the President of the United States, there are constraints, whereas part of the power of somebody like Kennedy or Gaddis is that they can write whatever they want. In Kennedy's case, that is to write a book on the decline of great powers that has huge influence, much more than anything written by any government official during that time.

Q: You seem to imply in the introduction to The Age of Terror *that the power of the thinkers consists in their capacity to conceptualize the debate and set the frame for discussing practical politics.*

T: Sure, and there are examples of that. But there are also examples of people in government who set the terms. Again, Kennan comes to mind, Paul Nitze, with NSC-68, comes to mind. Kennedy in some of his speeches set the terms of the debate, Ronald Reagan did the same. Nixon and Kissinger set the terms of the debate not so much in their pronouncements or the things that they wrote, but in the policies they developed and implemented – for example: détente and the opening to China.

It is rather harder – no matter how influential somebody is – to set the terms of the debate on the outside. You can have an influence; if you look at Charles Krauthammer, for example, who wrote an article at the beginning of the 90s called 'The Unipolar Moment' which became a canonical document of what became later known as the Neocon-view of the world.

Q: Setting the terms – does this also hold for the moral dimensions of politics? Is it the task of an authority somewhat outside everyday politics to keep watch over the moral aspects of governing?

T: Sure, there are examples, although morality – or let's call it global civics – unfortunately isn't a factor to the extent that many of us wish it would be. You might look at certain Supreme Court decisions – especially eloquent: Louis Brandeis, Stephen Breyer – that for years afterwards have shaped the way we think about those issues.

Q: Let's move up to the international level: Would you agree that there is a general consensus across political affiliations that the American version of democracy should be disseminated across the globe, and that controversy arises only as to how to go about this most effectively?

T: No, I wouldn't actually. Morality as such is a word of limited utility in this context. Legitimacy is maybe a better word when you're talking about governments, coupled, when societies of a whole are part of the discussion, with the concept of global civics, which I think is beginning to develop some substance and traction, especially if you look at the work that a Brookings colleague of mine, Hakan Altinay, is doing. The United States has built up over the years a degree of legitimacy in the eyes of the rest of the world as an arbiter of what is fair, what is right. However, I might add – not in a partisan spirit, but just objectively – that America's legitimacy has suffered considerably in recent years because US policy led to the perception that people on its behalf were behaving in an illegitimate way. I am thinking, for example, about things like Abu Ghraib. But let's hope that that turns out to be an aberration.

The United States is, in an important respect, unique among nations – although the French in particular might contest how unique our position is; it's unique in that we're a country that is based on a set of *ideas* as opposed to national identity pure *realpolitik*. We're what might be called an 'idea-state' rather than a Westphalian nation-state. And that is where morality comes in. If you look at the founding documents of the republic – the Declaration of Independence, the Constitution, the Federalist Papers – you will see that there is a lot of morality in there. There is a lot about what is the right way for individuals to behave, and what is the right form of government, and so on. That strain of *moralpolitik* – as you might call it – has always been present in American policy making, including American foreign policy making. When we get into trouble is when our actual actions and their perceptions by the rest of the world undermine our claims to morality.

Q: Who should try and reconcile these actual actions and the ideas behind them?

T: It needs to be a conversation. There is no single 'who'. It needs to be citizens, some of whom are self-described or described by people who may hand out labels as public intellectuals. It needs to be leading voices in the media, which can be columnists. And it certainly needs to be public officials as well.

Q: Mr. Talbott, thank you very much for your time.

T: You are welcome, and thank you.

Michael Walzer

Editor, *Dissent*
School of Social Science, Institute for Advanced Study
Princeton University, NJ

Q: Professor Walzer, what audience do you have in mind for your publications?

W: I've always thought that I was writing for what may be a mythic figure, the general reader, and not for a specifically academic audience. It is especially easy to do that when you're a political theorist. There is an academic political theory, of course, some of it pretty esoteric, especially in its postmodern versions, and there are political theorists who write for other political theorists, and there are political theorists who are interested only in political theory, and not in politics. But still, political theory is an opportunity to write about politics in a way that is accessible to non-academics, and that's what I've always tried to do.

Because we make our living in the academic world, we have to publish some of our stuff in academic journals, but I always write as if I am writing for *Dissent*. And then, if I feel that I need, for professional reasons, to publish in an academic journal, I just muddy the prose a little bit, and add a lot of footnotes, and then the same article can go into an academic journal. But mostly I try to write for the political public – those people who are engaged in politics, and have been to college. Those are the available readers. None of us reach a lot of them, but they are the people I hope I write for.

Q: The reason I bring this up is a quote I found on the dust-jacket of your book, and it says: "This isn't a book from the political left or the right that tells you what to think. It is a guide to help one think clearly about war, it is a practical guide for the world we live in." Is there an intention to educate in what you do?

W: If I think of what I am doing as political theory, then its purpose is to provide a more systematic way of thinking about some set of public issues. For me, just war theory is not in any way an esoteric doctrine. It is simply a more systematic presentation of the ordinary judgments that we make about the decision to go to war and about the conduct of war. The arguments I talk about in *Arguing about War* have been going on for a very long time in different idioms. Yes, I am trying to provide a framework within which people can argue, but I am also making specific arguments about specific wars.

Q: Why did you choose to focus on American foreign policy?

W: My book *Just and Unjust Wars* was conceived first during Vietnam; I was active in the anti-war movement before I had anything like a theory about just and unjust wars. In fact it was listening to myself talk at all those meetings that led me to think that there was something more systematic to say about these questions. And it is not only American wars. I seem sometimes to be in the business of giving grades to wars, anybody's wars. I get telephone calls from journalists that ask me to say something about Israel and Gaza, or about Afghanistan or Georgia. But, obviously, as an American citizen I am most engaged in discussions about when and where *we* should be fighting and how we should be doing that.

Q: Could you define the term 'public intellectual'? Do you still deem it appropriate today?

W: I guess so. There is a public debate that goes on continuously in democratic countries about domestic and foreign policy, and there are people who are regular contributors to that debate and who try to speak on different issues from some coherent perspective. Yes, those people are intellectuals and they speak in public, so they are public intellectuals. A lot of them are also academics because you can't make a living, or not many people can make a living, by being a public intellectual, and so the academy provides the material base for a lot of our intellectual debates. In the academy, in addition to all the insiders, all the scholars writing for other scholars, there are professors who aspire to speak to people outside, and yes, those are intellectuals.

Q: Is it a problem that most intellectuals are affiliated with universities, think tanks, or the government these days? Does this possibly strain their claim to act – at least to a certain degree – outside of purpose-driven constraints? Are they still critics with a distanced point of view? Does this situation influence the quality of their work?

W: The university is, it seems to me, the best possible base for intellectual work. The problem it presents for the public intellectual is the problem of maintaining some kind of non-partisan perspective in his or her classes, in dealing with students. That's very important and it is difficult, and there are clearly professors who let their political opinions shape their teaching – which is a betrayal of their students. But I don't think the material support that comes from the university poses any problems for your public activity when you cease to be a non-partisan academic and become a partisan citizen. The fact that you earn money in the university doesn't seem to me any more of a problem than earning money anywhere else would be. Once you go into government, however – which many academics have done, starting as advisors to candidates and ending up as members of administrations – then you cease to be an intellectual because you no longer have the distance from power that intellectual life requires.

I have written on the idea of critical distance. I don't believe that we have to exist at some great distance from the society that we live in and criticize. I argue that critical distance is measured in inches. But you need to have some distance, some detachment, specifically from power or, better, from the exercise of power. You don't have to be radically detached from the culture of your fellow citizens.

Q: The recent past has repeatedly been called 'postmodernity', a phase in history characterized by a prominent notion of relativism. What do you make of this claim? Is there a tension between claiming a certain truth and validity of one's intellectual position and this notion of relativism?

W: I have never encountered a consistent relativist. I think certain things are in fact relative to other things. That is a normal feature of intellectual and political life. But the notion that everything is relative in the sense that we can never claim that we are speaking rightly and truthfully – nobody lives by a doctrine of that sort. When I argue that the Vietnam War was unnecessary and therefore unjust, I am claiming that that's the right thing to say, the right judgment to make. What I don't claim is that I have any special authority to enforce that judgment. I am just a citizen making an argument. I want to make the best possible argument, and I think at this moment that I am making the best argument that I can make. But I don't claim any special authority because I am a professor or because I have written a book about just and unjust wars, I just want to be listened to with the same attention and respect that any other citizen wants.

Q: The American intellectual seems to have been in a difficult position from the very beginning, a situation defined by a tension of the sort I mentioned before: A need for critical distance from society, and at the same time, a desire to intervene. Over the years, the intellectuals' authority has repeatedly been described as declining because of an alleged incompatibility of these positions. Richard Hofstadter even states a fundamental anti-intellectualism in American culture. Would you say that the authority of intellectuals has increased again recently?

W: I haven't noticed that, no. First of all, what Hofstadter describes is certainly a real phenomenon in American politics. But I think anti-intellectualism is an intermittent feature of populist and democratic politics throughout history, in all countries. In peasant uprisings in medieval Europe, for example, the cry would go up: "Kill all the lawyers!" They, together with the priests, were the only literate people. The notion that highly educated people are part of the class of oppressors is a very common popular theme. The ruling ideas of the age are the ideas of the ruling class – that Marxist dictum was not new when Marx said it.

Maybe a certain class of intellectuals, experts really, has attained popular recognition. No presidential candidate can be without economic advisors, and economists have a lot of clout, and those economists who become public intellectuals do speak with an authority that people seem to accept. And maybe now there is a similar group of national security intellectuals, who have more authority than they would have had before the age of nuclear deterrence or before 9/11. But general intellectuals, without any specialized knowledge – I don't think we are in a different position than we were before.

Q: How do you perceive the relationship between the academic world and the world of practical politics? What is the balance of power like between the two?

W: There are an awful lot of academics who aspire to be advisors to the president, and there are political theorists who have played that role. One of them is William Galston. He is a very good political theorist – if there is a strain of Aristotelianism in American political thought, he would be one of its representatives. He was active in the first Clinton administration, he was a domestic policy advisor, played a very important role. Now he is back in the academy. Political theorists are relatively rare in the world of practical politics, but there certainly are a lot of professors of economics, international politics, and security studies who aspire to a certain kind of political role, a classic role: Like Machiavelli, they want to be the man who whispers in the ear of the prince. It is the advisor to the president, to the secretary of state, or defense, or the treasury.

I haven't had much occasion to play that kind of a role. I did travel for a while, I wrote some position papers for Gene McCarthy in 1968; I chaired George McGovern's task force on the Middle East in 1972 – to which he paid no attention at all. And that was the end of my experience with presidential politics. Most of us at *Dissent* think that, while we support particular candidates and would much prefer a Democratic to a Republican president, given any imaginable American administration, we would and should be critics.

Q: Why did you choose the position of an academic?

W: If there were an American social democratic or socialist party, I might have aspired to be the editor of its theoretical journal, if it had a theoretical journal. But there isn't anything like that in the United States. So for a political intellectual the only way to make a living – unless you have the ability to write best-selling books – is at the university, and maybe at some of the think tanks.

Q: Taking a closer look at the subtitle of your book Just and Unjust Wars, *'A Moral Argument with Historical Illustrations', one gets the impression that questions concerning morality are highly important for your work. How would you evaluate the issue of morality in politics?*

W: At the 75th anniversary of the Institute for Social Research in Frankfurt I gave a talk on – or maybe against – social theory. We used to have on the Left, or among left intellectuals, and especially in the Marxist tradition, a certain kind of world-historical theory. It started with the division of labor in ancient Babylonia and it went up to the latest strike by workers in Detroit. I remember meetings of the old Left where people would begin at the beginning, with the division of labor, in order to argue for these or those tactics for this strike in Detroit. But this wasn't a moral theory, it was a world-historical theory. We were the representatives of the progressive forces, and we *knew* what was right because we knew what was coming. We knew the course of world history, and since world history was tending to the creation of a Socialist or Communist society, all we had to do was to stand on the side of the advancing forces – or, even better, in the vanguard of those forces. And now none of us believe that. We don't have the guidance of a world-historical theory.

So where do you find guidance for left politics, or for any politics? My answer to that is that you find it, first of all, in morality. You make arguments about justice and injustice, oppression and liberation. We are no longer historicists, but we clearly are moralists. With regard to war, I suspect that it's always been the case that no political leader can send young men out to fight, to die, to kill in a war without claiming that this is the right thing to do. He has to make that claim to the parents of those young men. And so the discourse of war has always been a moral discourse. And that's why you can find arguments about whether to go to war, or not, in Thucydides, and in the Bible, and in Hindu literature, and Arabic literature, and everywhere. And also arguments about how to fight, whom you can kill and whom you can't kill – the argument about non-combatants is very old.

And in other fields, too: The argument about welfare and taxation – who bears the burden of taxation, who receives the benefits? Those are, they have to be moral arguments. How can you justify taxing this rich man at 35% of his income, and this poor man at 5% of his income, or not at all, without giving a reason – and this reason will have to appeal to ideas about justice and fairness. There is another way of arguing about public policy, and that is with regard to efficiency, the cost-benefit analysis that economists would do. But if you look closely, the identification of the costs and the benefits, and at the arguments about who pays the costs and who gets the benefits, these are often concealed moral arguments.

Q: Is it the task of an authority somewhat above the din of everyday politics to keep watch over moral issues? Especially in a case like war? Who should make sure that moral guidelines are adhered to?

W: In a democracy, it is up to the citizens. But I don't accept the argument that if the citizens of a democracy elect a president who fights an unjust war, they are all responsible, and all guilty, and an attack on them is not wrong anymore. That is the argument that some terrorist organizations make. Yes, democracy is a way of dispersing responsibility, it makes for the widest possible dispersal of responsibility. But responsibility is also, still, specific in important ways: Elected officials justly receive blame and credit for what they do – and most of the rest of us are innocent of blame and undeserving of credit. We want citizens to be engaged, and we encourage engagement with critical issues and participation in political processes. Certainly, we want them to criticize unjust wars. But that is a wish, not a command.

Q: Whom specifically do you have in mind?

W: The critics are anybody who joins in the critical work. Look back at the people in Britain who spoke out against the Boer War in South Africa. Look back at the people in Italy who opposed the attack on Ethiopia, the people in Germany who opposed Hitler or went into exile. They came from different walks of life. Criticism isn't the task of a particular group; it isn't an assignment. One of the extraordinary things about politics is how in a crisis people whose abilities were never recognized suddenly turn out to be able to organize a demonstration, or write a pamphlet, or make a speech – and then when the crisis is over, they go back to ordinary life. We lose sight of them.

Q: Would you agree that there is a general consensus among public intellectuals in the US – although they might have differing political affiliations – that the dissemination of American democracy is to be supported, and that controversies arise mainly as to how to proceed most effectively?

W: There is a notion that it is a good thing if American democracy is imitated or reproduced in other parts of the world. And that goes way back. Even among the founders, there was this radical idea that we would be – in the biblical phrase – "a light unto the nations." People around the world would just see the light and be astonished by it and then want to reproduce it. We wouldn't have to do anything except sit here and shine. Sometimes, though, there were ideas about helping – the Wilsonian idea, for example, which is rather a nice idea, that we should make the world "safe for democracy." We didn't have to make the world democratic, only to create a world order where, if people in particular countries wanted a democratic government, they would have a chance to get it. That's an attractive idea, I think. To make the world democratic in our image, and to use force to do it, that's an unattractive idea. And it is a much more recent conception.

Q: I would like to read a quote from the preface of your book Just and Unjust Wars. *You claim that "we urgently need a theory of just and unjust uses of force [...]. The immediate question for us is whether the permissions reach to regime change and democratization."*

W: And my conclusion is that they don't. But again, there are different positions from which one makes democratization arguments. Imagine that you are a member of the democratic Left, an activist or intellectual, then it would be quite natural for you, if there is a struggle for democracy going on in Uzbekistan, to express your solidarity with the Uzbekistanian democrats, maybe to raise money for them, to write articles on their behalf, to urge the United Nations to send investigators if the repression is brutal, and so on. That's a legitimate role. The goal is regime change, but the method is persuasion and material support, not military support. So from that perspective, I am a democratizer, my comrades are the people in other countries who struggle for democracy. But if I had political power, I wouldn't be justified in invading Uzbekistan – even if the regime is a brutal one – in order to create a government in my democratic image.

Q: What importance does the notion of American superpower have for the way the United States acts in the world? How should the United States go about in conveying its stance? In your 2006 preface to the fourth edition of Just and Unjust Wars, *you ask the question: "Is regime change a just cause for war?" Then you state that "[t]his is a question that is only indirectly addressed in* Just and Unjust Wars, *it seems right to deal with it now." Why now?*

W: Because regime change is being used to justify the war in which my country is currently engaged. And the hegemony that America for the moment enjoys in world politics does give American citizens and therefore intellectuals some added responsibility – because the deployment of our power has consequences for other people. But we – on the Left – aren't comfortable with that hegemony. So one of the things that I think American leftist intellectuals should be doing is – you can't be terribly influential doing it – telling people in Europe that we very much need a partner, a particular kind of partner, who can say yes and no to the United States. And that given the wealth, the economic clout, and the political potential of the European Union, there are also responsibilities on your side of the Atlantic – to think about how the world goes and ought to go.

Q: I would like to return to an issue of relevance for domestic politics. How would you evaluate the importance of public deliberation in American democracy? Where do you see the intellectuals in this process?

W: I have written a long essay on deliberative democracy; it is in *Politics and Passion*. I have never been a fan of the theory of deliberative democracy, although I am very close politically to some of the people like Dennis Thompson and Amy Gutmann who write about it. Maybe this is just a feature of the English language. Deliberation is what juries do. A jury is a group of citizens who have no interest in the outcome of the trial which they are adjudicating. They are literally impartial, non-partisan. They have been checked by the prosecuting and defense attorneys to make sure they have no family connections and no ideological connections with one or the other side. They deliberate until they reach a verdict – from the Latin for a 'true speech' – about what happened in this case. They are not allowed to do the things that politicians, legislators, party militants do all the time. They are not allowed to negotiate with each other, to bargain with each other. You can't say, "I'll vote your way on the first count of the indictment if you vote my way on the second count." You can't say that. Deliberation is a very special form of discourse – and a radically nonpolitical form. It is very attractive. In the last issue of *Dissent* we have a whole section on juries and jury service, a pro-jury set of articles. We start with Tocqueville's description of the role of the jury in American life and then we have eight accounts of jury service; we are very proud of this institution.

But politics is a different enterprise. In politics, people are not non-partisan, they are not disinterested. They have commitments, ideological commitments, material interests at stake. Politics can't be purely deliberative. You want people to argue with one another, you want them to make the best arguments they can make, you want them to appeal at least some of the time to the common interest. But it's not wrong for democratic citizens, when they are thinking about how to vote, to ask: "What's good for the steel workers, or for the state of Pennsylvania, or for the Catholics, or for the Jews?" Of course, you should also ask: "What's good for the country?" But the first questions are not ruled out in politics the way they are ruled out in deliberation. Politics is a partisan activity, the goal is to win. And sometimes it is very important to win. There is a lot at stake. And so the use of pressure tactics, of mobilization, demonstration, rhetorical exaggeration – all this is par for the course in politics. And public intellectuals are engaged in these activities. They aspire to eloquence because they want to be persuasive. They will look for allies, they will speak for a party or a movement in a way that a juror can't. So I think argument is important in politics, but deliberation is a non-political activity.

Q: Professor Walzer, thank you for your time.

W: Thank you, and good luck.

Cornel West

Class of 1943 University Professor of Religion
Center for African American Studies
Princeton University, NJ

Q: Professor West, you don't seem to be afraid in any way of cutting across different sections of knowledge and culture, and trying to bridge the gap between them while reaching out to a broad audience – as with your book Democracy Matters...

W: It cuts across the disciplinary division of knowledge in the professional managerial space called the academy. As I say over and over again, I am a blues man in the life of the mind, and a jazz man in the world of ideas.

What that really means is: You go back to Plato, Book Ten, 607b – the traditional quarrel between philosophy and poetry. It is really a fight between two forms of *paideia*, two forms of deep education. Homer is in place, Plato is trying to replace Homer. Homer represents the poetic. Here is this new conception of *paideia* rooted in the conception of philosophy. So we get the emergence of these two very different ways of turning the soul, cultivating the self, and engaging in what we call deep education. Now when you say 'blues man, jazz man', what you are really talking about is memory, history. You are talking about song, and trying to fuse mind, heart, and soul. For me then, in traditional terms, philosophy must go to school with poetry. And poets must wrestle with the philosophical. Walter Benjamin is crucial because – as Hannah Arendt said – he is a thinker, but he thinks poetically in a philosophical way. So there are people – in highbrow European tradition – where you can see that they are wrestling with that quarrel in such a way that the two are tied. For me, 'blues man, jazz man' means in fact that the two are tied. But the difference is what Ralph Ellison said: "The Blues is an autobiographical chronicle of personal catastrophe expressed lyrically."

You begin with the catastrophic. It could be indigenous peoples in Australia, it could be working class in Argentina, it could be peasants in

Italy, it could be Africans on slave ships – you begin with the catastrophic. And the question then becomes: Given that starting point, how does philosophy go to school with poetry against the backdrop of catastrophic circumstances? It is like the angel of history in Benjamin – piling of wreckage upon wreckage, and what is defined as progress for some is actually hitting against the wings, trying to somehow generate some motion. In that way, the old notion of disciplinary division of knowledge doesn't fall by the wayside, it just doesn't constitute an impediment in terms of one's quest for trying to get at these forms of *paideia* that is a force for good in the world.

Q: Is there an educational component involved in what you do? Do you intend to provide citizens with a framework of knowledge that allows them to participate effectively in democracy?

W: Absolutely. But again, I would continually use the word *paideia* – what the Germans used to call 'Bildung'. Now it has ideological uses, but what it really means in the end is that it is a vocation. This is very different from a profession. It is a calling, 'Beruf', as opposed to just a career, which means that you are trying – in the Jazz tradition – to find your voice.

In a sense, highly professionalized discourse just echoes. When you find your voice, that is the Nietzsches and Schopenhauers, that is the Humes and the Lockes. It is very difficult, but that is what you aspire to. For what? For a *paideia* for everyday people – that is the deep democratic twist. But against catastrophic circumstances – that is the Blues sensibility. So you are always already dealing with what Samuel Beckett calls 'the mess'. He says "Heidegger talks about being, Sartre talks about being, I talk about the mess." And the mess is all the wounds, and scars, and bruises, and how are we going to negotiate, and navigate, given that we are temporal beings, that we move from womb to tomb and not hear the alarm – how are we going to be a force for good and truth-telling?

The trajectory, especially within the West, goes back to the poets – not just Homer, but also Sophocles, and Plato: His hostility to poetry is primarily because of the false claim of the poet. He himself is a poet, he is using myth, all kinds of metaphors and narratives. And of course he began as a poet. He is fearful of poetry because he understands the strength and power of poetry. He is actually, in a certain sense, a kind of poet. People misread his exclusion of most of the poets as devaluing poetry.

No! That is an acknowledgment of its power. If he is going to get his project of *paideia* off the ground, he has got to somehow contain this stuff. The trajectory goes through Homer and Sophocles on to Lucian. The same is true for Erasmus, and David Hume. It is a humanist tradition that is fundamentally concerned with engaging the public critically, pedagogically, for the same purpose that Plato talks about in *The Republic*. He juxtaposes in Book 7 the twirling of the shell with the turning of the soul – pedagogic! The turning of the soul, for us, is from what hip-hop artists would call 'g-string and bling-bling' to truth and justice. From materialism, hedonism, narcissism, narrow individualism, to what kind of human being you really want to be. What about integrity? What about magnanimity? What about serving ordinary people? What about sacrificing for those who are suffering? That for me is the real core of the vocation.

Q: How would you define the term 'public intellectual'? Is it still an appropriate term these days?

W: Sure. But you always want to historicize, contextualize, and therefore pluralize any discourse about 'the public'. It has a history, it can be found in a variety of different places, and with different people who constitute the content, who are the constituents of publics.

The academy, for example, is as much a part of the real world as any other part of the real world. It is a public. A very important public. It has its own parochialism, and provincialism, but it has its own riches and virtues, too.

The churches, as a Christian, that is another kind of crucial public. The public constituted in democratic projects under rule of law, where you engage in public discourse, a discourse in which rights, and liberties, and responsibilities, and obligations play an important role.

Then there is youth culture. I spend a lot of time in hip-hop. That is a very important public. Most of them are unchurched. A lot of them are disengaged from the democratic public that is shrinking every day. A lot of them are far removed from the academy – a crucial public, but a public they hold at arm's length. But they have got their public, and it is a very powerful public. The question becomes: Given these different publics, how does one attempt to know enough, to be acquainted enough with the various vocabularies of each one? You have got to be exposed to the language, and the vocabulary. The same is true within the democratic public. One chooses which public one intervenes with.

Q: Let's turn from the present to the past: The situation of the American intellectual seems to have been a difficult one from the very beginning. It is a situation characterized by the tension of reconciling two different claims: A claim to intervene in society, and a need for critical distance from that very society so as to maintain 'impartial' judgment. What do you make of this claim to act outside of purpose-driven constraints, given the fact that the majority of intellectuals these days are affiliated with the government, the academy, or one of the numerous think tanks?

W: Critical distance is a very important thing to have. It is true for the great poets, the great philosophers, the great writers. The question is under what conditions does one find its critical distances operating?

Part of the challenge in the United States is the historical specificity about the emergence of U.S.A.: It is anti-colonial on the one hand – vis à vis Britain. It is deeply imperialist vis à vis indigenous peoples. It is slave-centered – 22% of the 13 colonies are enslaved Africans whose wealth production constitutes one of the fundamental pillars of the American democratic project. But it also has an inferiority complex vis à vis Europe. How do you confront and overcome and work through the inferiority complex – with Emerson being the grand figure – as an intellectual vis à vis Europe, given anti-colonial revolt against British empire, given the imperial expansion from 13 colonies to 50 states, given the heterogeneity of the population with the migration flow and so forth?

America has a very, very fragile national identity. And it tends to be pretty immature, adolescent, which is to say that it doesn't want to confront the nightside, its underside too directly. You can imagine someone like myself as a bluesman, beginning always already with the catastrophic circumstances – they don't want to hear that. They really don't. And it is only when they are at the brink of a real crisis or a disaster that the Frederick Douglasses, the William Lloyd Garrisons, the Elijah Lovejoys, the Harriet Tubmans are the voices you have to come to terms with. Because those catastrophic circumstances are now unfolding in such a way that they call into question your whole democratic project.

I come out of a tradition that fuses the Emersonian in terms of confronting the inferiority complex vis à vis Europe in saying "we understand that our very language is an extension of a European language, we don't have a Beethoven, we don't have a Hegel, we don't have a Goethe, Flaubert, Molière, or Montaigne." These are iconic figures in the history of the West – especially the modern West – that we Americans just don't have. We have our Melvilles, our Faulkners, and Toni Morrisons – but no Tolstoi! Dostoeswskii! This means – and this is where John Dewey is so important, in some ways even more than Emerson – that you are going to have to acknowledge what you do have, and work with what you have got. And try to find forms of excellence in democratic modes that are not always comparable to what Europe has to offer – so that in the end maybe Europe can end up learning from you, even though you are not going to have an American Tolstoi.

Q: Still, you seem to draw a line between the artistic and academic world on the one hand, and the political and economic world on the other. In your book, you state: "[I]t has been primarily artistic, activist, and intellectual voices from outside the political and economic establishments who have offered the most penetrating insights and energizing visions and have pushed the development of the American democratic project." Why would it be less problematic to be affiliated with a university than with the government, or a think tank?

W: My fundamental claim there is that the exercise of *parrhesia* – which is the free, plain, unintimidated speech that Socrates talks about in the *Apology* – is part and parcel of deep *paideia*. It takes courage. It is a real cause, you take a risk. The academy, especially in the United States – Harvard, Yale, Princeton, Johns Hopkins – thinks of itself as modernizing, but they generate subcultures that do not put a premium on courage. They put a premium on highly specialized modes of research and inquiry that reinforce conformity and complacency. The academy is wonderful in sustaining a tradition of research and inquiry, but the paradigms under which this takes place are not paradigms that are critical, engaging, let alone prophetic vis à vis the powers that be. The sixties are different because the social movements hit so powerfully that the academy is just completely discombobulated because of the fundamental questions that are asked and that have not been wrestled with by early American historians; this is what Allan Bloom is so concerned about.

The academy in the United States, although – unlike in Germany – not civil servants, are still on their own, and relatively autonomous, even though their funds are tied to the elites of the society. It is their money that allows them to flower and flourish. If working people, or black people, or women had to wait for the academicians to tell their story and to promote their cause, we would still live in patriarchal households, with the corporate elite power running amok because the academicians are so conformist. Although very smart, and very brilliant, very conformist. There are very few courageous academicians. It is almost as if you get socialized in paradigms in such a way that courage is never a principal part of the socialization – all the way up: Tenure, professorship, chair, university professor. Whereas you can't be a bluesman, or a jazz man without courage. It is impossible because you can't find your voice if you are not courageous. You will be an echo all your life, playing in some other lounge, echoing somebody else's music. Very nice technically, but you are not a jazz person in terms of aspiring to be that voice that all the great blues men and women attempt to be. This is why I tend to valorize artists and poets. There is always examples, also in the academy: Noam Chomsky, C.W. Mills, Sheldon Wolin, Howard Zinn, Martha Minow, Angela Davis, Edward Saïd, and of course bell hooks.

Q: A recent period of history has been dubbed 'postmodernity'. Broadly speaking, its predominant notion is relativism, meaning the non-existence of an ultimate, universal truth. What do you make of this notion as someone who has published a book like Democracy Matters, *which obviously makes a claim that what you have to say is valid and true?*

W: Relativism in its various forms is to be rejected across the board. There is no doubt that truth, no matter how unpacked or understood, has some crucial role to play. It's like when someone asked Josiah Royce why he talked about the absolute – is there such a thing as the absolute? And he said: "I just did a deed that can never be undone. That's absolute." He is right about that. There are certain realities you cannot *not* know, be it birth, death, being in love, out of love, or a child's sparkling eyes touching your soul. The crucial point is: There has to be an acknowledgment of a dynamic contextualism so that every truth claim put forward is dependent on a context. Simply because it depends on a context does not mean that it cannot be held to be true. It is just that you have to have a fallibilism in your contextualism: All of your truth claims are always open to revision because you could be wrong – that is true about black holes, it is true about this table, beauty, goodness, or whatever. But that doesn't mean that the quest, the search, the pursuit is not worthwhile, or that the claims that you make are not better than certain claims that others are making. Because there are certain better interpretations, of Shakespeare, of micronature.

So relativism is not really even a part of the discussion. I don't think anybody can live a radical relativism. Everybody knows that the death of your mother is more than the death of a fly on the wall. But that doesn't mean that any kind of sophomoric objectivism or transcendentalism hold. I am a historicist, but a historicist is a dynamic contextualist and a falli-bilist. There is a point to the relativist critique, but the conclusion cannot be relativistic. Remember the very beginning of *Negative Dialectics* by Adorno where he echoes the great insight of the Hebrew Scripture: "The need to let suffering speak is a *condition* of all truth..." For me, that is always the starting point. That is both an existential and a political truth. If you really want to know the truth of the society, then you ought to lis-ten to those Matthew 25 talks about: The least of these. The prisoners, the widows, the elderly, the workers, the homosexuals, those who have been marginalized and dejected. That doesn't mean that what they say is nec-essarily true, but you have got to hear their voices. They have to play a role in the conversation, in the quest for truth. When you cast it in that way, the truth about America requires that you have these voices heard – and it is going to be painful! Slavery. Lynching. Jim Crow. Jane Crow. Do you really want to hear that America? Most people would rather leave it aside. But this notion that would somehow downplay the genuine quest for truths for who we are as a human kind, as a nation – I have never taken that seriously. It has always struck me as a spectatorium. I have critical distance as a participant.

Q: Taking one last step toward the present, how do you evaluate the au-thority of intellectuals since 2001, that is, since the terror attacks of 9/11 and their aftermath? Is there a demand on the side of the American public for a guiding voice of reason that will explain the course of their nation to them?

W: In one sense, you are right. Anytime in a crisis, people are looking for a vision.

Q: In your book, you say: "We are at a rare fork in the road of American history." Whom do people follow?

W: It is true that intellectuals are included among those people looked to. But we have got a free-market fundamentalism that reigns ideologically in the right-wing hegemony of our day. Therefore, people are hungry, but many more are influenced by Bill O'Reilly or Sean Hannity who are not intellectuals, really. They are talking heads who attempt to speak to the needs of a crisis-ridden nation, and who themselves are pulling from intellectuals. The Neoconservatives who have been playing a fundamental role in the last thirty-five years are promoting the free-market forces that make it difficult for critical voices to emerge.

The Chomskys and the Zinns, they are not criticized. They are demonized. They are 'un-American', which is of course the last thing mainstream Americans want to hear. It trumps the debate, it cuts off any kind of dialogue with voices that are necessary and indispensable. There is another crucial role here, and it has to do with Jewish people. America is one of the few places in the history of the world where Jewish people have been allowed to flower and flourish – and I hope it continues. America is in that sense a kind of promised land. Given the tremendous stress on learning in Jewish culture, and given the magnificent emphasis on texts and the interpretation of texts, you in fact end up with a significant number of those in the intelligentsia who are Jewish, and who have complicated, fascinating, but crucial relations to Israel and Israel's intimate connection to the American empire. In the last forty years, it has become very difficult to engage in a critique of American foreign policy, American imperial power, and – in connection with the latter – corporate elite power at home. You try to be ethical and critical, but you get immediately demonized. Part of that has to do with the way in which the American intelligentsia is deeply influenced by viewpoints that make it hard, if not impossible, to critically engage certain kinds of American foreign policies. The people are hungry and thirsty, but they can't gain access to the voices for too long.

Q: What exactly are the people hungry for? Do they expect you to come up with concrete policy proposals? Or rather with a visionary framework of American ideals?

W: I think it is threefold.

First, more than anything else, they want truth claims regarding the narrative. How does the present relate to the past? Where does the present come from, how did it emerge? What are the conditions for its transformation? So first, it is the storytelling that is very important.

Second, the critique of what is in place. This is not the same as a narrative, even though the two are inseparable. They are not identical, but inseparable.

And third, a vision: Where are we going? How is that connected to policy, to political possibilities, and to presidential elections? In the end, you have to deal with political power, there is no doubt about that. The readership wants all three. In America, we have some towering progressive intellectuals. But they are so easily demonized as well.

Q: "The aim of this book is to put forward a strong democratic vision and critique, rooted in a deep democratic tradition..." This is a quote from the second chapter. In the course of the book, though, you become very specific, very practical about what it is you want to achieve, and why. So what is your main motivation?

W: It is really not that difficult to imagine what needs to be done. One percent of the population owning 51% of the wealth, corporate greed running amok, schools collapsing, 21% of our children living in poverty in the richest nation in the history of the world. It is not just a matter of moral disgrace, it is a matter of saying "we have got our priorities wrong." We don't have the political will to emphasize education, physical infrastructure, ecological balance, health care, and so forth. And we know it takes some kind of investment in these things: Moral, financial, and so forth. How come we don't have the will to do this? What is blocking the wheel? I don't think it is just a matter of people trying another project on our policy. It is a matter of a certain framework of understanding the present that generates the deliberate ignorance and the willful neglect – thinking that neglect and ignorance will not come back haunting you later on.

We have been here before, in a sense. But we had our priorities warped, and now we have got our priorities warped in this way: The militarism, the authoritarianism, the free-market fundamentalism. We have to understand ourselves in light of a different narrative, asking ourselves why we get into this right-wing period, and how to get out of this political ice age. How does this thing start to melt? You have got to get people to see – they have to become more awakened, more alert. Second, they have got to become more courageous, which means that they have to believe that it is possible. And third, they have to have some vision. And by vision, I don't mean some kind of technocratic projecting of a plan.

As a Christian, I take very seriously the prophetic tradition. My Christian faith is a footnote to prophetic Judaism: Justice is what love looks like public. That is a steadfast commitment to the well-being of others.

Justice becomes a matter of ensuring that 'the least of these' do not have their humanity violated, their dignity called into question. What forms that takes is hard to say. I am a deep democrat, so I believe deeply that democracy is what justice looks like in practice. But I am also very American. I do think democracy is a universal value that is applicable across cultures. But I have to be fallible enough, self-critical enough to know there is a variety of different forms of it. But everyday people, they have to have their voices heard in order to be treated with decency and dignity. That is what democracy in the end is about.

Q: You say it takes moral investment to bring about change. Who should watch over the moral aspects of politics? Is it the task of an authority who is somewhat outside the political trench warfare?

W: There is a wonderful line in Kant's *Critique of Pure Reason*: Examples are the go-cart of judgment. It is a Wittgensteinian moment in the text when he is talking about the fact that you can't appeal to a rule to teach you how to apply it. This is the difference between knowing 'that' and knowing 'how'. You know that the rule applies, but how do I know when to use it? Well, rule can't teach you that. It is a phronesis, it is practical wisdom. What does that mean? 'Examples are the go-cart of judgment' means that when we are talking about moral authority in democracy, we are not talking about being bestilled from on high. It has to come out of the examples and exemplars of everyday people who have extraordinary magnanimity that lures you and convinces and persuades you that that life is a life worth living. It is like with Martin L. King. Just take a look at his life. Just keep studying his life, and then, more than likely, in a democratic context, you are going to see things that are so attractive and appealing that you might reconsider and examine yourself. But it is a leap of faith, a Pascalian leap of faith in ordinary people.

Q: "Democratic practices – dialogue and debate and public discourse – are always messy and impure." As a citizen, where do you find your bearings? What is your point of orientation?

W: I bring so much baggage to the table.

First, a deep commitment to courage to think deeply and freely. That is what Socratic is. These Socratic sensibilities are part of my identity. Then the courage to love. It is a virtue that comes out of my tradition that I am less likely to give up. You can give up some other virtues like temperance and so on, but the one at the center is love, connected with justice. The third one is hope. That gives me a certain orientation. Given my conception of *paideia*, and given my concern about the underside and the catastrophic, and given my blues identity, the tragic-comic is for me the very means by which you get to hope. So there is a very threadbare conception of hope, it is no thick optimism at all. This is Beckett: Try again, fail again, fail better. This is my conception of hope, blueslike to the core. Those three baggages that I bring to the conversation give me an orientation that makes it difficult to ever fall into wholesale, paralyzing despair for too long, or to ever become so cowardly that you hate and pursue revenge rather than justice, or to give up on free inquiry and dialogue, and self-critical exchange. If someone were to ask me to give up on the Socratic, the prophetic, and the tragic-comic, they would be asking me to commit intellectual and existential suicide.

Q: Love, hope, the courage to think freely – these could be universal values applicable to everyone across the nation. If we look over the period that has passed since September 11 – a new situation for the nation, poignantly painful –, is it necessary to create a unifying myth for the nation? Or do you think the very existence of adversarial political camps generates competitive, prolific debate that will supply the best solution for all?

W: I wrestle with this with regard to my support for Barack Obama. I am a critical supporter of his. His calling is a calling of progressive governance. My calling is Socratic and prophetic.

The problem with myths is that they are never true, but true all the time. They can easily blur into lies that hide and conceal certain realities and truths that need to be confronted. Both have a therapeutic purpose, but myths tend to be more all-embracing so that you can confront the nightside. You can tell the fairy tale of Cinderella, and actually disclose some deep truths by telling those lies, just like a great novel. The fiction is there in order to get you to live your life better by examining who you are. Whereas lies themselves, without the larger mythic canopy around it, are very dangerous. The role of the Socratic and the prophetic intellectual is to expose the lies, and tell the truth, and bear witness. Take Chomsky's great definition going back to the 1967 essay of his where he was coming out of the academic shell, responding to American imperialism. He has been the great towering public intellectual, along with Edward Saïd, for the latter part of the 20th century.

So when you say 'uniting myth', I would say 'yes' and 'no'. There has to be a way in which our common humanity is accented so that we don't kill each other in the name of the truths that we are putting forward. On the other hand there can't be myths that are actually lies that allow an order to stay in place without really coming to terms with justice. That is a tight rope you have to walk. And it is why Socratic and prophetic intellectuals are always, in some sense, either marginalized or demonized. People are highly suspicious of them because when you pull the cover over those lies, a lot is at stake. People have invested in those lies. The notion that every generation in America gets better – that is just a lie. That doesn't mean Americans are demons, it just means human beings are all willfully ignorant and blind. You have to tease out these myths. There is regress, there is retreat in the history of America. We have made movements, and we moved back. Reconstruction – Jim Crow. Let's be honest about these things. We can celebrate the breakthroughs in the sixties – that is another move forward. And here comes right-wing hegemony. This is a setback for working people and poor people. So the question becomes: What does a Socratic, prophetic intellectual say in the light of a candidate he supports critically when he also has to succumb to the myths of the nation in order to gain access to the mainstream? It is a tight rope.

Q: So much for the tension within the American nation. What about America's relationship with the rest of the world? Would you agree that there is a general consensus among intellectuals that the American version of democracy should be disseminated throughout the world, and that the controversies revolve around how this dissemination can proceed most effectively?

W: We have to call into question the notion that there is one model of democracy, even within the US political discourse.

There is no doubt that the dominant model has to do with free market forces tied to elections, and maybe getting around to serious protection of rights and liberties. Whereas the model I would want to opt for – which I think is deeply democratic – is highly suspicious of unregulated markets, and elections in which the context of those elections remains unexamined, and where the vast economic inequality in place makes it difficult for voices to be heard, let alone rights and liberties thoroughly protected. I am a libertarian in terms of the centrality of rights and liberties. Any of the so-called leftist, progressive regimes that downplay rights movements, like

Cuba, I am highly critical of, even as I can applaud the developments in literacy and health care and poverty. Without rights and liberties, you still don't have the preconditions for democracy, let alone democracy itself.

So when I think of those dominant forms of democracy being exported, I am very critical because I can see that it does not mean that you have a deep commitment to democracy – by those Neoconservatives, Neoliberals, and others. The hypocrisy becomes overwhelming. None of them are worried about Saudi-Arabia, none of them are worried about Pakistan, regimes they prop up, where rights and liberties are crushed, or hardly exist. And they are crushing democracies, like Haiti. The question becomes: How do you go about defending and promoting deep democratic forces in other countries? Because I do believe that a democratic project does have an obligation to promote deep democratic forces. With the defense of Tibet against the imperial forces of China, we have a moral obligation to speak up, to defend the democratic forces against dictatorial elite. Just like we did in Vietnam. Just like we do in Iraq, or Zimbabwe. Does that mean that this is imperial, simply because you are transgressing national boundaries? Not at all. There is in fact a certain kind of universalizing activity that ought to take place when it comes to issues of decency and compassion. It has to be done in a self-critical way because you can still bring with you in your baggage American imperial arrogance: Knowing it all, condescension, hardiness, and so forth. But we still have a moral obligation to align ourselves with those forces. And a lot of times, it does cut across ideology. I agree wholeheartedly with William F. Buckley – a formative figure in terms of the right-wing hegemony – in terms of defending Jews in Russia, in defending all victims of Russian authoritarianism. My problem with him always was why he defended those folk, and yet defended Jim Crow, against King, against civil rights. What about consistency?

Q: How should America go about conveying this claim of promoting democracy?

W: It has got to be by example. In 1973, you had to be willing to step up and say: "We may not fully agree with Salvador Allende, but we oppose any attempt to anti-democratically overthrow his government." But we know there are other factors going on, and then the lies proliferate. Thank God there is Chomsky, and Saïd, and Barbara Ehrenreich, Naomi Klein, and bell hooks, and a whole list of those courageous intellectuals who try to at least go on the record as telling some very painful truths, and expos-

ing some vicious lies. But also bearing witness. Part of the problem of
many of the intellectuals is that they bear witness in their texts, but they
don't like to put their bodies on the line. There is a difference between
being a progressive public intellectual, and being an intellectual warrior.

Q: What exactly is the difference?

W: A warrior is always willing to put his or her body on the line. Martin
L. King was a warrior. Whereas most academic progressive intellectuals
– whose views are crucial and indispensable – are not warriors. There is a
certain streak of cowardice when it comes to bodily sacrifice. As for
black intellectuals, anybody who has told the truth about white supremacy
in America has always had to live under death threat. This is a different
thing. I had people trying to kill my wife. I had people showing up with
two shotguns in my driveway. I get threats every day. It is a different
state of being when you live with those threats all the time. It doesn't
make anybody a better person for being threatened. But how you deal
with those threats has to do with the quality of your courage. If you back
down – understandably – then it is clear you are not a warrior, you are an
academic progressive intellectual. You have to make a choice, though:
How are you going to respond? Will the response take the form of an anger that leads towards revenge, or the form of righteous indignation that
still puts the primacy of love and justice? That is why Martin L. King, or
W.E.B. DuBois, are such touchstones for black intellectuals.

*Q: So as a black intellectual, you must surmount even higher hurdles than
usual because of the color of your skin?*

W: On the one hand, being a black intellectual warrior and public intellectual is an advantage because the issue of race and white supremacy is so
crucial in the society that the mainstream press and others do want to hear
what black intellectuals have to say. So that my white intellectual comrades
who have much to say on a whole host of issues – their issues don't surface
as quickly. I get called more often, and therefore become more visible.

The flipside of that is to become so ghettoized, so circumscribed as if all
you have to talk about is just race and white supremacy – which one is
never in any way ashamed to talk about. But they look at a book like *Democracy Matters*, and they say: "He is talking about imperialism, democracy, empire, Emerson, Melville – I thought all he has got to talk about is
race matters."

Q: How do you get out of this pigeonhole?

W: You can't. It is like the blues artists: All you can do is sing the blues, and tell people to watch and listen for a while. You use the issues of race and so forth as a launching pad into a whole host of things, and you end up taking them to: What does it mean to be human? Is that a relevant enough question for you? And people don't think you can get from one to the other. All of us are caught in our historical moment. You are betwixt and between. You are on a tightrope, and there is no way to get off. Only when you die, you get that kind of freedom. So the fundamental question is: How do you use your death? Do you use that for love and justice? How are you going to use your death? Death has to be part of your life so that dying itself generates new effects and consequences that are democratic, compassionate and so forth. This is probably a question a lot of public intellectuals may not wrestle with that much. Howard Zinn probably does. He is such an activist, he probably gets threatened all the time.

Q: Finally, I would like to touch upon the issue of public deliberation. Your concern for the value of dialogue seems to create the frame for the whole book. At the beginning, you say: "[W]e are losing the very value of dialogue." And at the very end, you say: "[O]ur Socratic questioning must go beyond Socrates. We must out-Socratize Socrates by revealing the limits of the great Socratic tradition. [I]t has always bothered me that Socrates never cries – he never sheds a tear." How important is public deliberation for democracy? And where do you see the role of the intellectuals in this?

W: My conception of deep democracy does include not simply the Socratic stress on interrogating and questioning, but also the role of empathy – this is where the poets come in. P.B. Shelley talks about poets as the unacknowledged legislators of the world – all those who use empathy and imagination to get into the skin of other people and see what it is like to look at the world through their lens. For me, that is crucial in democracy. You have to open yourself to such a degree that your self-understanding is predicated on how you understand others. And you can't understand others unless you try to get outside of yourself. You empathize with others. You get out of that egocentric predicament.

Public deliberation requires a Socratic commitment to almost relentless interrogation and questioning, but also this cultivation of empathy and imagination. In the end, this is poetic because you are trying to somehow muster a conception of the world as beyond what you have at present, and then pit it against one another in a dialectic interplay – knowing that some kind of overcoming, 'Aufhebung', with elements of both is in the future. It is very much like Jazz. Find the courage to lift your voice. You can't find the courage unless others are trying to muster their courage to lift their voice. Your voice is dependent on their voice because you have got to listen to their voice to find out exactly how to pitch your voice, and together your voices fuse and generate new possibilities. So empathy is crucial.

The problem with Socrates is: If he never cries, he never really loves and empathizes. Does Socrates really get inside Thrasymachus's skin, or is he just responding to the argument? You have got to get inside to find out what is going on. If you have never loved, you have never really lived – you might have been a thinking thing, but never a full human being, with all of the tears, and the grief that go with it.

Another way of talking about this is the 12th paragraph of *The New Science* by G. Vico, where he talks about 'humando'. Humanitas comes from burying: The burial of the bodies in order for history itself to be generated because you don't want the petrified bodies to be there, unable to move through time. So there is a fundamental connection between loss, human, memory, and history. Part of the problem with Socrates is that he is usually ahistorical. He doesn't really have a deep sense of loss. All of us are dealing with loss. All the great poets – and their muses – are about loss. Empathy and love are intimately tied to loss. All loss is tied to grief. That is where the song comes from – the lamentation song is the first utterance having to do with wrestling with grief. Somehow you have got to memorialize. That is the history memory has got to come to terms with.

Q: So we might call the intellectuals the 'lead singers' for the rest of the nation?

W: The intellectuals are – if not the moral antennas – then at least the promoters of the singing *paideia* because we always want to link the song to the deep education. Which is where we started.

Q: Professor West, thank you very much for your time.

W: You are welcome. Thank you.

Howard Zinn †

Professor Emeritus, Department of Political Science
Boston University, MA

Q: Professor Zinn, what audience do you have in mind for your publications?

Z: I never write for a scholarly audience. I never write for my colleagues. I never write for professional historians. I always write for the general public. Probably, historians more and more are coming to think that way. Historians are beginning to think they should move outside the specialized audiences, the specialized readership, and speak to a larger constituency. But I have done that from the very beginning, maybe because I was a political activist before I was an academic. Therefore my objectives have always been political objectives. I was always interested in persuading people of my point of view, and reaching a larger public. So writing for such a public came natural to me.

Q: Is there a dimension of education involved in what you do? Do you intend to provide the American public with a frame of knowledge that will allow them to participate effectively in democracy?

Z: It is on my mind. Of course, the people who write foreign policy are writing from different points of view, and they have different ideas about what they want the public to think. But certainly, my idea is to present the public with ideas which they don't usually get from most books on foreign policy. Yes, that is my aim.

Q: The question came to mind when I read the following words in the first chapter of your book Passionate Declarations: *"How we think is not just mildly interesting, not just a subject for intellectual debate, but a matter of life and death. If those in charge of our society – politicians, corporate executives, and owners of press and television – can dominate our ideas, they will be secure in their power." This seems to be such a strong appeal to the reader and something more fundamental than making a single argument: The need to know what is going on.*

Z: That's right. If people do not really understand the roots of governmental behavior, as they do not adopt a critical view of what is going on, then they become victims of authority. They become victims of government, of government propaganda. They don't think for themselves. It is a matter of life and death because it is a matter of war and peace. If people are not prepared by understanding history to look critically at government policy, and as a result go along and collaborate with government policy, the result will be war, the result will be death to large numbers of young people. That's why I call it a matter of life and death.

Q: You just mentioned that you started out as a political activist. Later on, you held a position in the academic world for a long time. What do you think your readership expects from you – concrete policy proposals, or rather a visionary frame for the course of the American nation?

Z: I don't think they expect a specific policy proposal. They expect historical background, and a discussion of broad principles. Is there such a thing as a just war? What is the relationship between the individual and the state? What is the role of law, and what is the role of disobedience to law? Those are the things I deal with in *Passionate Declarations*. I may at times get close to specific policy suggestions, for instance, talking about economic justice: The role of government in assuring people the basic necessities of life. But mostly, I am trying to get people to think in broad terms about the principles that could guide them in understanding the world.

Q: Your book is entitled 'Passionate Declarations'. You once said: "It is impossible to be neutral on a moving train." There seems to be such a strong moral appeal in your work. How do you evaluate the discussion of moral aspects of politics? Is it the task of an authority somewhat beyond the fray of everyday politics to remind us of morality?

Z: I insist that all political discourse is fundamentally a moral issue. There is no way of avoiding judgments. Ultimately, all discussions of political theory and history come down to the effects of these principles and policies on human beings, so they are all moral issues. When historians – or scholars of any field – claim that they are not really dealing with moral issues, that they are just being objective and presenting information, they are just deluding themselves and their readers. I make this clear in the early part of my book: There is no such thing as simply describing reality. When you describe reality in a certain way, that description is always from a certain point of view, and therefore it has moral implications.

Q: You seem to go even further, though. In your preface, you state: "The power of determined people armed with a moral cause is, I believe, 'the ultimate power'." So morality can influence the reality of politics?

Z: Yes, because I think in order for citizens to affect history, in order for them to play a role in history, they have to be moved by a moral cause. We would not have an anti-slavery movement in the United States before the Civil War unless people were moved by the moral issue of slavery. It is the moral issue that gives the passion and the power to a citizens' movement. You might say it helps compensate for the fact that they don't have military power or financial power. To be strengthened by a moral principle creates a special power for people which enables them at certain times in history to overcome the power of authority.

Q: Who is going to bring in the moral principle? Who is supposed to set the citizens' movement into motion?

Z: We all have that responsibility. I don't think there is any *one* group. Marx said it would be the working class, but that is too narrow, especially since the nature of the working class has changed over time. It would take a combination of many, many different kinds of groups in the United States. But groups which are all outside of the temptations of the establishment. Groups that in some way have a grievance, or if they don't have a grievance themselves, that empathize with the grievance of others. They may not themselves be in danger of going to war, but they empathize with people who have to go to war. They are the ones who will have to organize a movement to bring about change.

Q: How do you perceive the balance of power between the practical-politics establishment and the academic world?

Z: The academic world has too long been outside the realm of political action. It has always been assumed that the academic world stands above that. That is why when people in the academic world become passionately involved in a cause, and in fact direct their scholarship and their teaching toward moral and political ends, they very often get into trouble because they are going against the tradition of the academy. But there has always been a minority of academics who think that the academy should be a place for critical thinking and acting. There has always been a conflict inside the academy between those who want to remain aloof from political engagement, and those who think the university, the college should actually be an ideological and political battleground.

Q: I would like to quote from your last chapter: "New definitions of old terms could become a part of the common vocabulary. The old definitions have misled us and caused monstrous harm." Would you say that academia has the power to conceptualize a political debate? In this sense, the academy would hold some power over the world of practical politics.

Z: I think that is a function that people in the academy can serve. Because they are scholars, and students, and thinkers, and readers, they have the ability to educate the larger public to examine more critically the language and concepts that are used by the politicians and the mass media. As an academic and a critical scholar, you have the opportunity to say "let's look at this phrase 'national security' and how it is used. Let's examine it. Let's look at this idea of obedience to law. Let's look at Plato and his insistence that Socrates must go to his death in order to obey the state which has nurtured him." The academy is a good place to really examine critically these various ideas and concepts.

Q: Is this the reason why you chose a position in the academy?

Z: Yes, exactly. I didn't choose it to become a professional historian, or in order to become a scholar, and to produce works for my colleagues and for scholarly journals. I was an activist before I entered the academy, I was a shipyard worker, I was in the Air Force, and I was already politically active and engaged. So when I went into the scholarly world, I knew that I was going to direct my scholarship toward political change.

Q: How would you define the term 'public intellectual'? Is this a term that still points to something relevant today?

Z: Sure. There are intellectuals who do not go out into the public to express their ideas, but who stay within their own scholarly circles. And then there are intellectuals who cross over into the real world. The ones who cross over are not always of one political persuasion. They range across the spectrum. They are intellectuals who go out into the public and serve the interests of the establishment. Henry Kissinger or Zbigniew Brzezinski are such examples of public intellectuals. And then there are public intellectuals who become the opposition, the dissidents. So on the one hand, there is a division between a public intellectual and an academic intellectual, and then – among the public intellectuals – there is a whole spectrum of different opinions.

Q: Another feature of public intellectuals might be a certain tension that is possibly inherent to their role: On the one hand, a need for detachment and autonomy in order to judge matters of society in a comparatively unbiased way. On the other hand, a desire to critically intervene and exert influence. What do you make of this claim to act somewhat outside of purpose-driven constraints given the fact that the majority of intellectuals these days are affiliated with universities, the government, or a think tank?

Z: There is always a tension. But as soon as people decide to become part of the political struggle, they have declared that they are not going to claim to be objective and unbiased. They will still claim that they will tell the truth and not deceive people. But there is no doubt that in this tension, they have made a decision on the one side rather than on the other. A decision on the side of "yes, this is my point of view, and I declare it openly."

Q: Would you say that the authority of intellectuals has increased over the last years – since September 11, 2001 – contrary to claims of a decline in their importance and a general anti-intellectualism in American life?

Z: I agree with you on that. I think Hofstadter and others probably exaggerated the decline of influence because they were affected by McCarthyism and the Red Scare. There was a certain amount of timidity, and withdraw, and fear. But I think 9/11 has brought the public intellectual out more strongly and broadly than before because what the United States has been doing in the world is so dramatic, so important, has such consequences that it is hard for an intellectual to avoid getting involved in the discussion and wanting to play a part. The stakes are larger since 9/11 than they were before. There is more engagement on the part of intellectuals with what is going on.

Q: Is this a good or a bad thing? In your book, you talk about experts and the dangers of dependence: "To depend on great thinkers, authorities, and experts is, it seems to me, a violation of the spirit of democracy. Democracy rests on the idea that, except for technical details for which experts might be useful, the important decisions of society are within the capability of ordinary citizens."

Z: You know, there are experts, and there are experts. There are the experts who become part of the establishment, and they are the ones that we should fear because they give a kind of intellectual authority to terrible policies. The 'bright' men around John F. Kennedy during the Vietnam War, the Best and the Brightest, they gave a kind of authority to the Vietnam War. He had Harvard and Yale Ph.D.s and Phi Beta Kappas advising him and L.B. Johnson on the war. Those experts were dangerous to the public and to democracy. I don't call myself an expert, but for people who are dissidents and critics of existing policy, the idea is not to lead an ignorant public into certain directions but to try to educate the public in such a way that the citizens themselves become aroused. In others words, so that democracy is enhanced, not crippled.

Q: What about democracy in terms of foreign policy? Would you agree that there is a wide consensus across most political camps that the American version of democracy should be disseminated throughout the world, and that controversies only arise as to how to proceed most effectively with this dissemination?

Z: I think there is a division of opinion. There are intellectuals who go along with the idea that the United States should spread democracy in the world. Among these intellectuals, there are those who think it should be done by force, and then there are others who think it should be done by other means. There is a consensus among them that this democracy should be exported. The distinction between those who believe in doing it violently and those who don't is not absolutely clear because there are liberal intellectuals – or people who consider themselves Liberals – who won't believe in the intervention in Iraq, but they believe in the intervention in Bosnia, or in Afghanistan. They will disagree about where to use the military, but they will both agree that it is alright at certain times to use the military to advance democracy. And then there are those other intellectuals – among whom I include myself – who do not believe that it is the right of the United States to impose its democracy on the rest of the world, especially since we are very dubious about how democratic our country is. In other words, we question even the fact that we have a democracy to export. That is a very important difference among intellectuals.

Q: Given these doubts, how important is it in your opinion that the United States maintains its position as the only superpower in the world?

Z: It is very important that the United States does *not* maintain its position as superpower in the world. The very idea of a superpower which imposes itself on other countries, whether militarily, or economically, or politically, is abhorrent to the idea of a democratic world. Expanding the idea of democracy from the nation to the world, thinking that one country should dominate the world – these are violations of the democratic idea. That doesn't mean that I believe that the United States should be isolated from the world. It should play a role in the world. It should in fact be willing to use its wealth to help people in other parts of the world. But that is different from being a superpower which assumes dominance and supremacy.

Q: In the 'Ultimate Power' chapter, you discuss an image of American power that is being conveyed to the world, mainly through demonstrating frightening military might. And you ask the question: "What good has that image done, for the American people, or for anyone in the world?" What is the ideal image the world should have of America?

Z: The ideal image the world should have of America is that of a country that will not go to war anymore. A country that will not militarily intervene in other countries. There might be instances where the United States might be part of an international body of peace keepers, such as the role it might have played in Rwanda in the 1980s. But that is not making war, that is a different kind of peace-making intervention and mediation among different parties. The picture that I would like people all over the world to have of the United States is that of a country that is peace-loving. That does not have military bases all over the world, that does not send its troops or warships all over the world. That instead uses its resources to help people in other parts of the world, to send them food and medicine, to help them in their natural disasters. When things like tsunamis, hurricanes, or earthquakes happen, and American resources are tied up in wars in Afghanistan and Iraq, and there are not enough helicopters to rescue people from floods because the helicopters are at war in the Middle East – this power that the United States has can be used for good as well as for evil.

Q: My concluding question comes back to a feature of domestic politics: public deliberation. How do you evaluate the importance of public deliberation as a feature of democracy?

Z: We certainly are desperately in need of public deliberation. Our main problem with public deliberation is the control of the media, and the control of the educational resources, the control of television and radio. We need a public deliberation which is a true free market of ideas, and not a controlled market of ideas. But the deliberation itself by the public is absolutely essential. I believe if there had been a free deliberation by the public at the time the United States went to war in Iraq, and the public had not been bullied and dominated by the ideas of the establishment, and the government, and the press, then we would not be at war in Iraq. Public deliberation is absolutely essential if it is a democratic – and free – deliberation.

Q: In the 'Free Speech' chapter, you say: "National security is safer in the hands of a debating, challenging citizenry than with a secretive, untrustworthy government." Where do the intellectuals come in; what is their function?

Z: The role of the intellectuals is to make sure that there is a broad spectrum of facts and ideas available to the public for its deliberation. Public intellectuals should make sure that the discussion is not narrowed, not limited to the confines that are created by the establishment. So the public intellectual has the job of saying to the public: "When you think of the word 'security', you must not think only of military security, you must think of economic security, and social security. And when you think of 'democracy', you must think not just of an American brand of democracy, but of a more open-minded idea of what democracy can mean." In other words, it is the job of the public intellectual to enlarge the scope of citizens' thinking.

Q: Professor Zinn, thank you very much for your time.

Z: Sure, and good luck with your work.

Bibliography

1. Interviewed Authors: Selected Publications

1.1   Benjamin R. Barber
       Consumed. How Markets Corrupt Children, Infantilize Adults, and Swallow Citizens Whole. New York: W.W. Norton & Company, 2007
       Fear's Empire. War, Terrorism, and Democracy. New York: W.W. Norton & Company, 2003/2004
       The Truth of Power. Intellectual Affairs in the Clinton White House. New York: W.W. Norton & Company, 2001
       Jihad vs. McWorld. How the Planet Is Both Falling Apart and Coming Together and What This Means for Democracy. New York: Crown/Random House, 1995

1.2   John Bolton
       Surrender Is Not An Option. Defending America at the United Nations and Abroad. New York: Threshold Editions, 2007

1.3   Zbigniew Brzezinski
       Second Chance. Three Presidents and the Crisis of American Superpower. New York: Basic Books, 2007
       The Choice. Global Domination or Global Leadership. New York: Basic Books, 2004

1.4   Noam Chomsky
       Failed States. The Abuse of Power and the Assault on Democracy. New York: Henry Holt and Company, 2006
       Hegemony or Survival. America's Quest for Global Dominance. New York: Henry Holt and Company, 2003/2004

1.5   Jean Bethke Elshtain
       Sovereignty. God, State, and Self. New York: Basic Books, 2008
       Just War Against Terror. The Burden of American Power in a Violent World. New York: Basic Books, 2003

1.6   Francis Fukuyama
       America at the Crossroads. Democracy, Power, and the Neoconservative Legacy. New Haven and London: Yale University Press, 2006

State-Building. Governance and World Order in the 21st Century. Ithaca: Cornell University Press, 2004

1.7   Robert O. Keohane
        Power and Governance in a Partially Globalized World. London and New York: Routledge, 2002
        International Institutions and State Power. Essays in International Relations Theory. Boulder, CO: Westview Press, 1989

1.8   James M. Lindsay
        [with Ivo H. Daalder:] *America Unbound. The Bush Revolution in Foreign Policy.* Hoboken, NJ: John Wiley & Sons, Inc., 2005
        [with Henry J. Aaron and Pietro S. Nivola:] *Agenda for the Nation.* Washington: Brookings Institution Press, 2003

1.9   Michael Novak
        No One Sees God. The Dark Night of Atheists and Believers. New York: Doubleday, 2008
        The Universal Hunger for Liberty. Why the Clash of Civilizations is Not Inevitable. New York: Basic Books, 2004

1.10   Joseph S. Nye
        The Powers to Lead. Oxford: Oxford University Press, 2008
        Soft Power. The Means to Success in World Politics. New York: Public Affairs, 2004
        The Paradox of American Power. Why the World's Only Superpower Can't Go It Alone. Oxford: Oxford University Press, 2002

1.11   Clyde V. Prestowitz
        Three Billion New Capitalists. The Great Shift of Wealth and Power to the East. New York: Basic Books, 2005
        Rogue Nation. American Unilateralism and the Failure of Good Intentions. New York: Basic Books, 2003

1.12   Anne-Marie Slaughter
        The Idea That Is America. Keeping Faith With Our Values in a Dangerous World. New York: Basic Books, 2007
        A New World Order. Princeton: Princeton University Press, 2004

1.13   Nancy Soderberg
        [with Brian Katulis:] *The Prosperity Agenda. What the World Wants From America – and What We Need In Return.* Hoboken, NJ: John Wiley & Sons, Inc., 2008
        The Superpower Myth. The Use and Misuse of American Might. Hoboken, NJ: John Wiley & Sons, Inc., 2005

1.14   Strobe Talbott
        The Great Experiment. The Story of Ancient Empires, Modern States, and the Quest for a Global Nation. New York: Simon & Schuster, 2008

[with Nayan Chanda (Eds.):] *The Age of Terror. America and the World After September 11.* New York: Basic Books, 2001

1.15   Michael Walzer
        Just and Unjust Wars. A Moral Argument With Historical Illustrations. New York: Basic Books, 1977/2006
        Politics and Passion. Toward A More Egalitarian Liberalism. New Haven: Yale University Press, 2005
        Arguing About War. New Haven: Yale University Press, 2004

1.16   Cornel West
        Brother West. Living and Loving Out Loud. A Memoir. Carlsbad and New York: Smiley Books, 2009
        Hope on a Tightrope. Words and Wisdom. Carlsbad and New York: Smiley Books, 2008
        Democracy Matters. Winning the Fight against Imperialism. New York: Penguin Books, 2004

1.17   Howard Zinn
        A People's History of the United States. 1492-Present. New York: Harper Perennial Modern Classics, 1980/2005
        Passionate Declarations. Essays on War and Justice. New York: Harper-Collins Publishers, Inc. 2003
        Terrorism and War. New York: Seven Stories Press, 2002

2. Further Reading

Bauman, Zygmunt. *Legislators and Interpreters.* Cambridge, UK: Polity Press, 1990

Elster, Jon (Ed.). *Deliberative Democracy.* Cambridge, UK: Cambridge University Press, 1998

Furedi, Frank. *Where Have All the Intellectuals Gone? Confronting 21st Century Philistinism.* New York: Continuum, 2004

Hofstadter, Richard. *Anti-intellectualism in American Life.* New York: Vintage Books, 1962

Jacoby, Russell. *The Last Intellectuals.* New York: Basic Books, 1987

Kritzman, Lawrence (Ed.). *Michel Foucault. Politics, Philosophy, Culture. Interviews and Other Writings 1977-1984.* New York: Routledge, 1988

Kuklick, Bruce. *Blind Oracles. Intellectuals and War from Kennan to Kissinger.* Princeton: Princeton University Press, 2006

Melzer, Arthur M., Jerry Weinberger, and M. Richard Zinman (Eds.). *The Public Intellectual. Between Philosophy and Politics.* New York: Rowman & Littlefield, 2003

Posner, Richard A. *Public Intellectuals. A Study of Decline.* Cambridge: Harvard University Press, 2001

Small, Helen (Ed.). *The Public Intellectual.* Oxford: Blackwell, 2002

Troy, Tevi. *Intellectuals and the American Presidency. Philosophers, Jesters, or Technicians?* New York: Rowman & Littlefield, 2002

Short Biographies of the Authors

Benjamin R. Barber is Walt Whitman Professor of Political Science Emeritus at Rutgers University. He is the president of CivWorld at Demos, an international NGO based in New York City, and its annual Interdependence Day event. Barber has been an outside adviser to President Clinton and has consulted with German Presidents Herzog and Rau, the Liberal Party of Sweden, and the European Parliament. He holds a Ph.D. from Harvard University and has taught at the University of Pennsylvania, Princeton University, and the University of Maryland, among others. Barber received the Palmes Academiques (Chevalier) from the French government and the Berlin Prize of the American Academy of Berlin. He appears frequently on television, including *The Tavis Smiley Show*, *The O'Reilly Factor*, *CNN International*, and *Charlie Rose*. His plays have been produced off-Broadway in New York, and he speaks German and French fluently.

John R. Bolton, a diplomat and a lawyer, has served in several Republican presidential administrations. From 2001 to 2005, he was Undersecretary of State for arms control and international security, and from 2005 to 2006, he served as the U.S. permanent representative to the United Nations. Bolton is a senior fellow at the conservative American Enterprise Institute (AEI), a think tank based in Washington, D.C. His area of research is U.S. foreign and national security policy. A regular *Fox News* commentator, Bolton is involved with the National Rifle Association and the Council for National Policy, among others. The son of a Baltimore firefighter, he lives in Maryland.

Zbigniew Brzezinski is a counselor and trustee at the Center for Strategic and International Studies (CSIS) in Washington, D.C., and the Robert E. Osgood Professor of American Foreign Policy at the School of Advanced International Studies, Johns Hopkins University. From 1977 to 1981, Brzezinski was national security adviser to President Jimmy Carter. In 1981, he was awarded the Presidential Medal of Freedom. Brzezinski holds a Ph.D. from Harvard University and honorary degrees from Georgetown University, Williams College, and Warsaw University, among others. He appears frequently as an expert on the PBS program *The News Hour with Jim Lehrer*. Born in Poland, Brzezinski is married to Czech-American sculptor Emilie Benes. Their son Mark has also served as an adviser to both Presidents Clinton and Obama.

Noam Chomsky is Institute Professor & Professor of Linguistics Emeritus at the Massachusetts Institute of Technology (MIT). Considered one of the fathers of modern linguistics, Chomsky established himself as a prominent critic of U.S. foreign policy during the 1960s when he opposed the Vietnam War. Since then, he has been an outspoken political commentator; his social criticism also includes an analysis of the mass media. A member of the Industrial Workers of the World, Chomsky is considered the 'most cited living author'; the Arts and Humanities Citation Index also ranks him the eighth most cited source of all time, trailing Marx, Lenin, Shakespeare, Aristotle, the Bible, Plato, and Freud.

Jean Bethke Elshtain is the Laura Spelman Rockefeller Professor of Social and Political Ethics, Divinity School, The University of Chicago, with appointments in Political Science and the Committee on International Relations, and holder of the Leavey Chair in the Foundations of American Freedom, Georgetown University. A political philosopher and the recipient of nine honorary degrees, she grew up in a tiny village in northern Colorado and was the first woman to hold an endowed professorship at Vanderbilt University. Elshtain holds a Ph.D. from Brandeis University and is a contributing editor for *The New Republic*. In 2006, she was appointed by President Bush to the Council of the National Endowment for the Humanities. Elshtain is married and the mother of four children.

Francis Fukuyama is senior fellow at the Foreign Policy Institute at the Paul H. Nitze School of Advanced International Studies (SAIS), Johns Hopkins University, and the Olivier Nomellini Senior Fellow at the Freeman Spogli Institute for International Studies at Stanford University. Fukuyama is also chairman of the editorial board of *The American Interest*. His book *The End of History and the Last Man* has appeared in over twenty foreign editions and made the bestseller lists in the United States, France, Japan, and Chile. Fukuyama holds a Ph.D. from Harvard. In 1981-82 and in 1989 he was a member of the Policy Planning Staff of the US Department of State. Fukuyama is a part-time photographer and has a keen interest in early-American furniture, which he makes by hand.

Robert O. Keohane is Professor of International Affairs at Princeton's Woodrow Wilson School. Keohane holds a Ph.D. from Harvard and has received honorary degrees from the University of Aarhus, Denmark, and Science Po in Paris. He has taught at Stanford, Harvard, and Duke University, among others. In 2005, *Foreign Policy* ranked him the most influential scholar of international relations. A former president of the American Political Science Association, Keohane is married to Nannerl Keohane, herself a noted political scientist.

James M. Lindsay is Senior Vice President, Director of Studies, and Maurice R. Greenberg Chair at the Council on Foreign Relations, New York and Washington, D.C. During the Clinton administration, he was director for global issues and multilateral affairs at the National Security Council. Lindsay holds a Ph.D. from Yale. He has contributed articles to the op-ed pages of many major newspapers, including the *New York Times*, the *Washington Post*, the *Los Angeles Times*, and *The Australian Financial Review*. Lindsay and Ivo H. Daalder won the 2003 Lionel Gelber Prize for *America Unbound* which was chosen by *The Economist* as one of the best books of 2003.

Michael Novak is a theologian and author. He has served both Republican and Democratic administrations since 1972 and was U.S. ambassador under Ronald Reagan for three missions. Novak wrote speeches for John F. Kennedy and Robert Kennedy and was invited to lunch by John Paul II. In 1994, Novak received the Templeton Prize for Progress in Religion (a million-dollar purse awarded at Buckingham Palace), and delivered the

Templeton address in Westminster Abbey. He currently holds the George Frederick Jewett Chair in Religion and Public Policy at the American Enterprise Institute in Washington, D.C., where he is Director of Social and Political Studies. His writings have appeared in every major Western language, and in Bengali, Korean and Japanese, and he has received 28 honorary degrees.

Joseph S. Nye, Jr., University Distinguished Service Professor, is also the Sultan of Oman Professor of International Relations and former Dean of the Kennedy School of Government at Harvard University. Nye holds a Ph.D. in political science from Harvard. He has served as Assistant Secretary of Defense for International Security Affairs, Chair of the National Intelligence Council, and Deputy Under Secretary of State for Security Assistance, Science and Technology in the Clinton administration. The 2008 TRIP (Teaching, Research, and International Policy) survey of 1700 international relations scholars ranked him the sixth most influential scholar of the past twenty years, and the most influential on American foreign policy. Nye coined the term 'soft power' in the late 1980s.

Clyde V. Prestowitz, Jr. is founder and President of the Economic Strategy Institute, Washington, D.C. He served as counselor to the Secretary of Commerce in the Reagan Administration and played key roles in achieving congressional passage of NAFTA and in shaping the final content of the Uruguay Round. Before joining the Commerce Department, he was a senior businessman in the United States, Europe, Japan, and throughout Asia and Latin America. Prestowitz regularly writes for leading publications, including the *New York Times*, the *Washington Post*, *Fortune*, and *Foreign Affairs*. He is fluent in Japanese, Dutch, German, and French.

Anne-Marie Slaughter is the Bert G. Kerstetter '66 University Professor of Politics and International Affairs and former Dean of the Woodrow Wilson School at Princeton University. She is presently on leave, serving as Director of Policy Planning for the United States Department of State. Slaughter is also the former President of the American Society of International Law and has served on the boards of the Council on Foreign Relations, the New America Foundation, and the Canadian Institute for International Governance Innovation. She has been a frequent commentator on foreign affairs in newspapers, radio, and television. Raised in Virginia by her American father and Belgian mother, Slaughter received her law degree from Harvard Law School and her D.Phil. degree in international relations from Oxford University.

Nancy Soderberg is a Distinguished Visiting Scholar at the University of North Florida and President and CEO of Soderberg Global Solutions. From 1993-97, Soderberg served as the third ranking official of the National Security Council at the White House. In 1997, President Clinton appointed her to serve as Alternate Representative to the United Nations as a Presidential Appointee, with the rank of Ambassador. Soderberg achieved international recognition for her efforts to promote peace in Northern Ireland and also advised the president on policies toward China, Japan, Russia, Angola, the Balkans, Haiti, as well as on a variety of conflicts in Africa. She is a regular commentator on national and international television and radio, including NBC, ABC, CBS, CNN, BBC, Fox News, and National Public Radio.

Strobe Talbott is president of the Brookings Institution, Washington, D.C. His immediate previous post was founding director of the Yale Center for the Study of Globalization. Before that, he served in the State Department from 1993 to 2001, first as Ambassador-at-large and special adviser to the Secretary of State, then as Deputy Secretary of State. Talbott entered government service after 21 years with *Time* magazine; he has also written for *Foreign Affairs*, *The New Yorker*, *The Economist*, the *New York Review of Books*, the *Washington Post*, and Slate. Talbott holds honorary doctorates from the Monterey Institute, Trinity College, Georgetown University and Fairfield University, and he has been awarded state orders by the presidents of Estonia, Finland, Germany, Lithuania, Poland, and the Kings of Sweden and Belgium.

Michael Walzer is Professor Emeritus at the Institute for Advanced Study, Princeton University. Currently, he is a Fellow of the Straus Institute for the Advanced Study of Law & Justice at the New York University School of Law. Walzer is editor of *Dissent*, a contributing editor to *The New Republic*, and a member of the editorial board of *Philosophy & Public Affairs*. He has taught at Princeton and Harvard and is a member on the Board of Governors at Hebrew University, Jerusalem. Walzer has written about a wide variety of topics in political theory and moral philosophy including political obligation, just and unjust war, nationalism and ethnicity, economic justice and the welfare state. In 2008, Walzer received the Spinozalens, a biennial award for ethics in The Netherlands.

Cornel West is the Class of 1943 Professor in the Center for African American Studies at Princeton University. He holds a Ph.D. from Princeton University and has taught at Yale, the University of Paris, Haverford College, Harvard, and Princeton. His book *Race Matters* has become a contemporary classic, selling more than half a million copies to date. The winner of numerous awards, including the American Book Award, West has also received more than twenty honorary degrees. He advised presidential candidates Al Sharpton and Bill Bradley, and offers commentary weekly on *The Tavis Smiley Show* from Public Radio International (PRI). West was an influential force in developing the storyline for the *Matrix* movie trilogy and has served as its official spokesperson, as well as playing a recurring role in the final two films.

Howard Zinn was a historian, playwright, social activist, and Professor of Political Science at Boston University. He died in 2010 at the age of 87. Zinn was a shipyard worker and Air Force bombardier before he went to college under the GI Bill and received his Ph.D. from Columbia University. He taught at Spelman College and Boston University and was a visiting professor at the University of Paris and the University of Bologna. His book *A People's History of the United States* has sold nearly two million copies to date. Zinn's memoir, *You Can't Be Neutral on a Moving Train*, was also the title of a 2004 documentary about his life and work.

Index

The new Journal
Politics, Culture & Socialization

PC&S publishes new and significant work that report on current scientific research, discuss theory and methodology, or review relevant literature. It welcomes the following types of contributions on topics which fall within our aim and scope:

Politics, Culture
and Socialization

Research   3/2010
Theory
Methods
Book reviews

- Empirical research articles
- Theoretical articles which analyze or comment on established theory or present theoretical innovations
- Methodological articles
- Book reviews

Issue 3
Vol.3/2010
Barbara Budrich Publishers
ISSN 1866-3427

The journal is published four times a year for an international audience. It relies on a wide range of subjects, compiled by scholars from around the world.

Editors: Prof. Dr. Christ'l De Landtsheer (University of Antwerp, Belgium), Prof. Dr. Russell Farnen (University of Connecticut, USA), and Prof. Dr. Dan German (Appalachian State University, USA).

Rates: Individual subscription (print) 59.00 €, (print + online) 69.00 €; institutional subscription 100.00 € (for institutional online, please contact publisher (josef.esser@budrich.eu); reduced rates (students, members of certain IPSA RCs) (print) 49.00 €. Postage added.

Verlag Barbara Budrich • Barbara Budrich Publishers
Stauffenbergstr. 7. D-51379 Leverkusen Opladen
Tel +49 (0)2171.344.594 • Fax +49 (0)2171.344.693 • info@budrich-verlag.de
US-office: U. Golden • 28347 Ridgebrook • Farmington Hills, MI 48334 • USA •
ph +1.248.488.9153 • info@barbara-budrich.net • www.barbara-budrich.net

www.barbara-budrich.net